Contents

On The Cover:
We asked Keith Weesner to illustrate a famous Hop Up Scene for Volume III. Fittingly, he chose this lakes image featuring the Hop Up 200 MPH Club trailer. Fitting, because Hop Up is now the sponsor of the 100 MPH Club for flathead four-bangers.

HOP UP CONTRIBUTORS
MARK MORTON — Publisher/Editor   DREW HARDIN — Managing Editor

JIM AUST, JOHN BADE, MIKE BISHOP, JIM CHINI, ROB FORTIER, JON GOBETTI, KEN GROSS, STEVE HENDRICKSON, FRED HILDAGO, AARON KAHAN, DAVE SIMARD, ANDY SOUTHARD JR., DARRYL SPURLOCK, AUSSIE STEVE, JIM STROUPE, DR. MARK R. VAN BUSKIRK, PETER VINCENT, KEITH WEESNER

COCO SHINOMIYA/MONSTER X @ HEY POSER INDUSTRIES — Art Direction

Indicia
Hop Up Volume 3 is published by **Hop Up Products**, LLC, dba Hop Up Magazine, P.O. Box 790, Riverside, CA 92502. All rights are reserved. No part of this publication may be reproduced without prior written consent of the publisher. Quoting of brief passages for the purpose of review is permitted. Printed in the USA, of course. ISBN 0-9675570-2-X

Mort's Shorts

*I*t's in the gut. An aura. A feeling. The visceral.

It's an unspoken cool that is the commonality among Hop Up Guys: Guys (and Chicks, too) who share the style of correctly done traditional rods and customs and race cars and scooters and...yeah, even planes or trains. You know when something is right. It's maybe understated. Maybe it's not painted. It has a vibe that you feel in your belly. But it's got the stuff, in performance, sound, look. It's our definition of cool. You guys yourselves are...just cool.

Not butterin' you up, either, because you knew it all along.

This annual attempts the impossible, which is to articulate what it is about our agreed style that cannot be articulated. It will be represented in photos and sketches and scrapbooks, and in sometimes halting, uncertain words. You can kind of hear the contributors saying, in a frustrated tone, "Ya know?" after a shot at putting it in words. This book may help you to know.

But ya gotta be born with the exponents. You have to have a genetic pre-disposition to cool or you won't get it. All the components are there for everyone, but Hop Up types organize the data, and it results in the kinds of cars that appear in the following pages, and a kind of behavior which is the self-assured, knowing execution of tricks of the old craft and the un-bragging peace that that execution brings us. More obtuse B.S., I agree, but isn't it difficult to describe what it is that's in your heart, and gut, and in your shop?

Oh, yeah.

They say "Living well is the best Rivenge."

The shop.

See, the shop is an important part of the culture. You have to have a shop or aspire to a shop or at least have respectful awe of them. You know that the shop is the sacred space where not much has changed since the Winfields and Gerbers, Chevrolets, Dryers and Horns (yes, Jim, even Horn) performed their hot rod alchemy. That space may be as simple as a bench with a worn-out vise and an old metal toolbox with some inherited tools. Or a lot more. Hop Up Guys understand the juxtaposition of the shop and the Iron. And the tools. Ahhhhh, the tools! But that's a topic for another day.

Here in Volume III we have the task of stating what cannot be stated, the salvation for which is that, what we have here is for the few. It's a fairly small cut of hot rod mankind that is focused as narrowly as we. It's a narrow focal point, but the essence runs deeper, with a kind of conviction that a guy feels in his, well, his gut. Well. Back to square one!

There are no "nouveau" Hop Up fans because you gotta have time in grade to feel the way we do. We welcome you to Hop On, read, look and enjoy. And we welcome you to throw in with us. But this is not a starting point. It's a destination. You have to have started somewhere else and evolved to here. And it's not that this is a higher state of evolution. Far from it. It's just that a certain set of genetic, cultural and environmental circumstances has to have occurred or none of this will figure for you. Having been on that journey, you may see what follows, shake your head, grimace, and know that finally, you have been defined.

That happened to me when I first saw Don Montgomery's *Hot Rods of the Forties*. And for that revelation. Thanks, Don.

Rods & Customs

Rods and Customs. They're the reason we'z here, Boys.

The feature section in *Hop Up 2002* reflects what Hop Up Guys in this millennium are doin' with the clues, the style, the craft that we inherited from those coots way back in the last century. They really had it goin' on, and if we're not too far off our mark, Hop Up Cats today got it goin' on, too. But the aesthetic *does* show some evolution.

Elsewhere in *HU 2002* Mike Bishop points out that we now build them safe and functional. If your eye is keen you will see that most of these pieces *sit* a little cooler than the ones 50 years ago; they might accidentally employ radial tires (not really a crime, now, is it?) and the odd alternator may be in charge, or even (rarely) front disc brakes might be hidden under a fender. But not on a highboy. No. Not on a highboy.

The customs are going to show our take on *that* genre, too: use old styling clues on old cars, and save the new tricks for late models.

We will see in what follows the full range of design approaches, from patinaed beater to painted, plated, trimmed and rimmed, and observe that in either one of those extremes, the Hop Up Guys might just as likely have switched roles with one other. The beater guy can *afford* to do a slick one; the slick guy has the founding and rod-intellect to do a bone-yard piece. They just did it the way they willed.

Gawd, this is a great job. And a great hobby.

Naw. It's a great *life*.

RIGHT PLACE RIGHT TIME

STEVE LEMMONS' '32 3-WINDOW FORD COUPE

By Peter Vincent

Steve Lemmons has a perfect example of a late Fifties/early Sixties full-fendered hot rod, right down to the original orange paint on the body and rolled and pleated upholstery. The stars lined up for Steve in finding and purchasing the coupe, and he also found the perfect person to put it all together. It was a case of being in the right place at the right time all the way around.

Steve bought the car from Skip Ziegler, who had purchased the car from Pete Eastwood, who bought the car from "some guy around the Stockton [California] area." That was Doug Ives, who now lives in Reno. Doug bought the '32 back in 1965, when he was 18 years old, from Don Canalupe. Don had purchased the car as a stocker in 1954; and in 1958 he converted it to a hot rod by putting in an engine, transmission and rearend from an almost new, but wrecked, '57 Chevy. He's the one who painted the 3-window orange, and it has stayed that color to this day. Doug had the car in his possession for 32 years and had blown it apart for a rebuild. But when he went through a

Original 60's Orange paint, Wimbledon White steelies, Vinther built nerfs and the occassional primer spot... all as it should be.

AUTHORIZED
PARKING ONLY
UNAUTHORIZED VEHICLES
IMPOUNDED
HERB'S TOWING
845-6750

From the top: Steve's '32 profiles and has a perfect stance; original early 60's rolled and pleated interior matches the theme; 327-inch power and full headers.

divorce and a move back to Nevada, he sold it to Pete in '97, who sold it to Skip, who sold it to Steve. Follow?

Steve talked to Bill Vinther about putting it all back together, and as we said earlier, timing was in his favor. Bill had just finished building a shop/garage, and after he and Steve talked over the project, they decided that Bill would be interested in following the coupe's direction and concept—an early-Sixties-style hot rod. Bill's realm is early-Sixties-styled cars. He knows what works and what doesn't within the time period. Steve and Bill laid out a plan for a "bare bones" styled '32 with small headlights, nerf bars, drum brakes, chrome garnish moldings and a 327 Chevy with full headers.

When Doug Ives blew the car apart in the Eighties, he had primed the fenders, grille shell and gas tank. But since Steve and Bill wanted to keep the original orange, Bill had to match the color that was still on the body. Bill built a new chassis using the original frame, which he boxed, plumbed and set up with a dropped I-beam front axle connected

Nerf bars, Pontiac taillights, trunk handle, and again, the occassional primer spot.

to a reverse-eyed spring with a shortened main leaf and some Pete Eastwood-built hairpins. The 3.70:1 narrowed Ford 9-inch rearend was mounted on a de-arched spring. The body was left stock, other than removing the cowl lights and adding sealed-beam headlights to the "Eastwood dropped" stock headlight bar. Bill crafted an impeccable set of nerf bars on the front and spreader bars for the rear, and added all of the hand-crafted brackets necessary to make everything work on the frame.

The 327-inch Chevy engine is a classic early Sixties choice. It's hooked up to a Turbo 350 transmission for easy and comfortable driving. A '41 Ford steering column, wheel and column shifter work the tranny and the Vega steering box. The 15x5-inch front steel wheels are mounted with 165/15 Michelins, and the 15x7-inch rears are mounted with 255/70R15 BFGoodrich tires. The wheels are all painted Wimbledon White, with small mid-Forties caps added.

The Wimbledon White was a perfect choice to set the car off, and it matched the white (almost ivory) portion of the interior.

The 1950 Pontiac taillights were already on the car and were left in their original location. The seat that was in the car when Steve purchased it was left as is. He took the car to Jim Almer in Longview, Washington, to match up the new door panels, kick panels, headliner and carpet. Jim also installed a new top insert and reinstalled the '49 Mercury door and window handles to match everything up. Bill added a set of Sanderson headers and hand built the rest of the exhaust. The original orange lacquer paint on the body looks perfect and has the right amount of "patina."

The '32 Ford is perfect as it is. If you could see underneath the car you would find some very nice detail work and subtle pinstriping added in the appropriate areas. Steve keeps getting asked if he's going to paint the car. No way, folks. It's done. 🚗

A DREAM OF A DEUCE!

By Jon Gobetti

When Washington state hot rodder Steve Lemmons began dreaming of a nostalgic roadster, he knew exactly what he wanted. Ford's Model 18 became an instant icon when it debuted on March 31, 1932. The "Deuce," as it's affectionately known, created quite a stir among southern Californian hot rodders. Their hard-core enthusiasm was based less on its beautiful lines than its revolutionary 221-cubic-inch, 65-horsepower, flathead V-8 engine. This valve-in-block engine created a thirst for speed, gave birth to a new industry, and dominated the era of dry lakes racing. The introduction of the more powerful, overhead-valve engine in the late Forties modernized hot rodding. This new engine helped transform the performance industry into the multi-million-dollar market that still thrives today.

That's why there was no question in Steve's mind that his Deuce roadster would reflect the spirit of late Forties hot rodding. "I kept looking at all those pictures in Don Montgomery's books, the ones taken at the dry lake runs and Bonneville. I wanted a late Forties/early Fifties look with a small-block engine and modern running gear."

Steve called on the talents of Roger Simonatti to help him combine the traditional and contemporary components that would provide the nostalgic looks and modern reliability he was looking for. Roger began assembling a So-Cal chassis using a transverse leaf spring, tube shocks, and hairpin radius rods that support and square a dropped I-beam front axle. Hydraulic brakes from a 1955 Ford pickup haul the highboy down from highway speed. To keep the Deuce to the right of the double yellow, Roger adapted Vega cross-steering using a '40 Ford column and steering wheel. In the rear, an additional transverse leaf spring, ladder bars, and shocks camouflage a narrowed, late-model 9-inch Ford differential and brakes.

A 327 small-block Chevrolet fed by a Hot Rod Carburetion Tri-Power system resides

Top to bottom: Steve Lemmons' black highboy roadster epitomizes the traditional pre-WWII era of hot rodding; original hood clamps hold the four-piece, Rootlieb NOS hood in place. Lighting the way is a pair of Arrow headlights mounted to a set of So-Cal brackets that pull double-duty as shock mounts; a 327 late-model small-block Chevy fed by three twos is actuated by a progressive linkage system. Polished early script valve covers add to the engine's timely appearance.

under the four-piece, Rootlieb hood. The complete package rolls on a set of 16x4-inch '40 Ford wheels up front, and 16x5-inch '59 Ford pickup rims at the rear, shod with blackwall Firestones. Trim rings with Ford button caps further punctuate the traditional theme.

Turning his attention to the body, Steve had only one thought: Steel! A call to Brookville Roadster produced some interesting facts. Yes, steel bodies were available, but there was a long waiting list. Steve's project would grind to a screeching halt while production orders ahead of his were filled. Not wanting to wait, Steve inquired about the availability of a disassembled body. Within days, all the panels needed to assemble a complete roadster body were delivered to Steve's front door.

Donn Lowe assembled the body, rounding and contouring the cowl to match the top of the doors. Within the steel dash he installed an old Mooneyes chrome panel with a machine-turned fascia. Five Stewart-Warner winged gauges fill the panel and monitor engine vitals. A 2-inch-chopped windshield protects both driver and passengers from the elements. A pair of $10 swap-meet Arrow headlights and reproduction '50 Pontiac taillights complete the package. Stan and Mike Dietz applied a deep, rich coat of black enamel. Jim Almer stitched up a handsome tan leather interior accented by wool carpets. The result: a dream of a Deuce with the best of both worlds, traditional looks combined with modern reliability. 🚗

Top to bottom: A simple chrome spreader bar protects the gas tank, while reproduction '50 Pontiac taillights reside in the lower rear body panel. Note Steve's choice in personalized plates; Steve replaced the original radiator cap with a bull nose that enhances the Ford logo; an old Mooneyes chrome panel with a machine-turned fascia resides within the steel dash. Five Stewart-Warner curved glass, winged gauges fill the panel and monitor engine vitals.

Lance Miller's
3-WINDOW COUPE

Lance does things thoroughly. Purely. His coupe had to be munged-up in the appropriate way, with period-perfect pseudo-accessories, appointments and components. It had to be one that the "Out of Touch Guys" wouldn't get. It had to be one that Hop Up Guys do get.

They do, Brother.

As you can see in these photos that we got here, it's the perfect, subtle, understated hot rod: '53 DeSoto Hemi, '39 box, banjo rear end. Black tires and black wheels on a (kinda) black car are a huge statement—if you're listening carefully. There's a covered seat but no top insert. Yeah, he can afford one, but just doesn't need one. There are perfect—yeah, frickin' perfect—fenders and boards hangin' in the barn, but he just doesn't need them. At the moment.

They might find their way on there some time or other. Who knows? These things always evolve. No hot rod is really done, is it? Ours certainly aren't.

We met up with Lance, his Brother Brad (in the cool primered '41 truck) and what is this? Yeah, their Dad's '43 Ford Jeep with a '49 Merc flattie in it. That's another story entirely. Maybe for Volume IV.

And we cruised Redlands, California, as it is, was, and should be.

Redlands was one of those destinations for railroad execs and industrialists and

Above: Understated? Yes. But oh-so-perfect in it's own way.

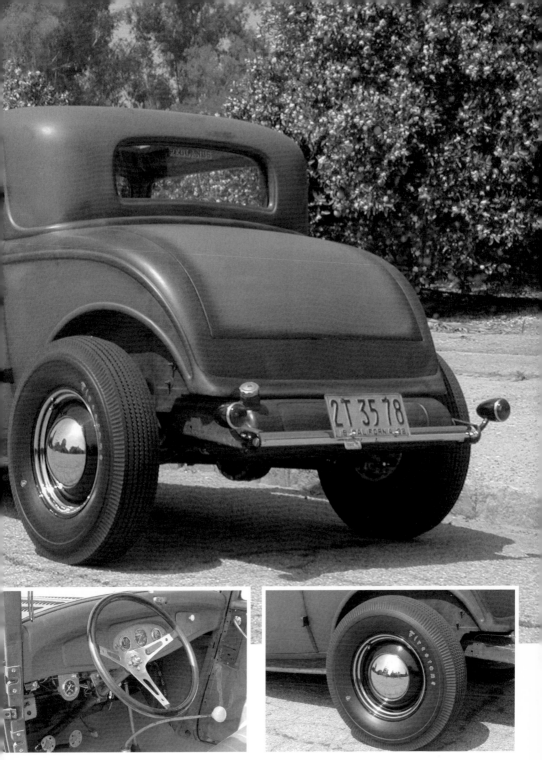

Top: How would you improve on this? A quick change? OK. It's being assembled now! **Bottom** (left to right): Home-made hot rod is obviously well-planned, tight and, well...Hot; austere to a fault, a monument of restraint. keep it simple, stealthy, and you, too, will know this kind of fun.

such after the turn of the century (that'd be LAST century, Boys), where they'd hang out while the weather was inclement in points North and East. The bucks they spent there stayed, and modern Redlands refuses to let the character escape, thus, a bad-ass area for cruisin' mansion-lined streets and genuine orange groves and, like that.

We'd stop now and then, get the story on the area from Lance. One of the stops was alongside another of the remaining (and perpetually protected by the city) orange groves, so we took some pictures to share with you. It was supposed to be a "photo shoot" anyway, but turned out to be way more "tour" than "shoot."

We had a great lunch (thanks) and bull session, went on a nostalgic tour in some consarnedly fine old iron, and, although both Brad and Lance are Hop Up Guys and River City Reliabilty Run regulars, got better acquainted with them. Finally met the Main Miller, Norm, patriarch of the bunch. The Brothers are cool, but Norm? Hey. We should grow up so cool.

Lance's car was the coupe du jour, but his kinfolk made for two new file folders in the ol' Hop Up "to do" box.

It's like findin' money, Boys. 🚗

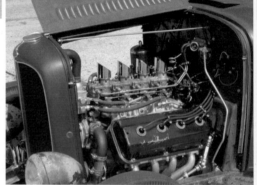

From the top: Miller family has it goin' on. Jeep is a Lake Arrowhead Chris-Craft fender running a feisty flathead; four 81s are functional. Lance is the chief carb man, keeps it in tune himself; headlights have since been replaced with black ones with even better patina. We'd take these!

Why do we do this thing called hot rodding?

To push the performance envelope?

To test our abilities and skills?

To make our products the best they can be?

To be a part of an American tradition?

Yes.

The Most Respected Name In Performance Air Conditioning
Call 800 862 6658 for a catalog or for your nearest dealer

The JIM KHOUGAZ ROADSTER

Written by Dr. Mark R. Van Buskirk

Photos by Dave Simard

You know how it is. Sometimes you put something away, meaning to get to it later, and never do. Well, this "something" was a car that time almost forgot. After sitting for nearly 45 years in the Van Nuys, California shop of Jim Khougaz, this channeled Deuce roadster was purchased in 1996 by Dr. Mark Van Buskirk and brought to his home in Indiana.

Khougaz was a member of the Outriders and later was a founding member of the Roadmasters. He built the roadster in 1946 for competition at El Mirage dry lakes, and he campaigned it there extensively through the early '50s. The car also competed in the 1949 Pasadena Reliability Run, coming in fifth.

Khougaz, who has the proof in a toolbox full of timing tags and memories, raced the car with a de-stroked crankshaft in 1950, where he went 122.78 mph in the "B" modified roadster class. His fastest time was 141.95 mph at the July 1949 SCTA meet at El Mirage in the "C" lakester class.

As with many dry-lakes cars, this roadster was raced with many different combinations of speed equipment, though the Mercury block was a constant. These variations are documented in the SCTA programs, which usually listed the engine type and displacement, as well as the type of cam, cylinder heads, intake manifold and ignition.

The roadster was channeled 7 inches, and the frame was Z'ed in the rear to get it super low. A '46 Ford rear with 3.54 gears was mounted in the frame, and up front a big beam '32 axle was dropped 3 inches and installed using a split '40 Ford wishbone with reversed-eye spring. Steering was through a '32 box mounted on the top of the frame rail. The roadster was also fitted with a full aluminum belly pan.

Inside the cockpit was a complete Auburn dash with a full set of Stewart-Warner gauges and a fuel pressure pump. The windshield was chopped three and a half inches, the body finished in a medium blue, and the front end was chrome plated.

The grille shell and insert were shortened 2 inches and a custom hood was fabricated with louvered hood sides. According to Khougaz, the guy who punched the hood side louvers missed one on the driver's side,

Top to bottom: The guys are qued for their next dusty run; wonder if the above run cost him a clutch?

and since it was a last-minute job, he accepted it with this flaw. It turned out that the missing louver helps identify the car in vintage pictures.

The car appeared in two early issues of *Hot Rod* Magazine. In February of 1949, it was featured as one of the hot rods in an article titled "Hot Rods vs. Sports Cars," where it competed on an oval track (notably against Phil Hill driving an MG). In the July 1949 issue, Walter Woron pictured the car as an example of channeling in his "How to Build a Hot Rod" series.

Jim Khougaz's son had thoughts of rebuilding the roadster in the Sixties, but little beyond the disassembly took place before the roadster once again was placed in storage. Now fast-forward 30 years. Dr. Mark Van Buskirk was considering building a '32 roadster when an ad in *Hemmings* for

Khougaz' '32 piqued his interest. During an instant trip to California, Mark snapped up the car and had it shipped to its new home.

Van Buskirk's next stroke of good fortune was meeting noted automobile journalist and hot rod expert Ken Gross at Motor City Flathead in Dundee, Michigan. The proprietor, Mark Kirby, had just completed the SCoT-blown flathead for Ken's gorgeous '32 roadster. When Van Buskirk mentioned to Ken that he was looking for someone to resurrect the Khougaz roadster, Ken recommended Dave Simard of Massachusetts-based East Coast Custom.

A weekend road trip brought the car to the Simard's east coast shop. The flathead will be assembled by Mark Kirby, and hopefully this second collaboration of these two fine craftsmen will be ready to roll in 2002. 🚗

Top to bottom: Roasters set to cruise the 'Hood; "before" shot—the car has a lot of character; "during" complete restoration at East Coast Custom.

NORTH COU *Sleeper*

NTRY

On the outside, this little green '40 is Clark Kent. Under the hood, it's another story.

By Ken Gross
Black & White Photos By Peter Sukalac,
Color Photos Courtesy Bob Ames

Summer of '55: I was 14 and an enthusiastic *Car Craft* reader, along with *Hot Rod* and *Rod & Custom*. I always recognized a new cover when I saw one, and the August 1955 *CC* cover was a beaut! It featured a cherry red flathead with a polished SCoT blower, twin shiny 97s, chromed water hoses and considerable wizardry in the meticulous way the fuel and vacuum lines had been coiled to absorb vibration.

A neat-looking finned compressor (for an alternative set of louder highway horns) perched behind the generator, and a slim, scratch-built air cleaner topped the carbs, fed by a length of 4-inch black flexible hose that extended down below the engine and out for fresh cold air. Chromed headers rounded out the engine. The stock heads matched the engine's red, and each of the 48 head studs was capped with a chrome cover. In a word, it was gorgeous.

To my surprise, in a story entitled "Bell Tel Boomer," the snazzy engine nestled under the hood of a plain Jane '40 Ford Standard business coupe. Although the car's builder, Dan Kilcup of

Top: Nothing much out of order here. The partially shaved deck and '49 Chev license plate guard are clues, but hey, single exhaust, factory height...gotta be a stocker, right?; **Bottom**: Kilcup reupholstered the tired '40's interior in premium tuck 'n' roll brown Co-Hyde, fitted a Stewart-Warner five panel under the dash and cleverly rebuilt the seatback so it would tilt for easier rear compartment access.

Portland, Oregon, had removed the blue trunk lid Ford V-8 badge, and relocated the license plate to a '49 Chevrolet surround on the stock bumper, he'd left the decklid handle in place. In front, the plate was also relocated and supported by another Chevy surround. He'd added a second chevron taillight (can you believe on a Standard in 1940, you still only got one taillight?), and that was about it for exterior changes.

Curiously, the coupe wasn't lowered, and one of the photos revealed a single exhaust pipe in the factory location. Still, this stock-looking '40 had made the cover of *Car Craft*, so there had to be a story here. Peter Sukalac, a frequent *Car Craft* contributor, shot the photos and wrote the copy. "Bell Tell Boomer" referred to the fact that Kilcup had purchased the coupe four years earlier from Ma Bell, where it had seen workaday service for 11 years. The purchase price had been $350, and Dan's ulterior motive was to refurbish the dented but sound Standard for his wife.

Peter Sukalac's text is typical of the period: "If the car was to be driven by the little woman, it naturally should be neat, clean

and mechanically reliable, mused Dan on arriving home. So the first thing to do was to have a body man iron out the wrinkles. This was easier said than done, however for all the 'tin bangers' shied (sic) away from a bid on the work. 'Too old,' said one; 'Can't be done,' said another; 'Nothing left to work on,' said still another. 'Nuts!' replied Dan, 'I will just do the job myself.'"

Kilcup got a little carried away. He sandblasted the body (unusual in that era), removed "every little wrinkle," and subsequently shot it with 62 coats (you read that right) of Lynton Green lacquer. Why so many? "It just kept getting better looking all the time," said Dan. "Besides, I wanted the surface just like glass."

The coupe's interior received the full treatment too. The old broadcloth upholstery was removed and replaced, along with the original door glass, window channels and weather stripping. The seatback was cleverly hung on spring balances for easy access to the rear storage compartment. An unknown trimmer (perhaps handy Dan himself) redid the seats in brown Co-Hyde (a

Top: The mild-looking coupe's engine room is crammed with machinery: supercharger, air horn compressor, remote oil filter, Vertex mag on an angle drive, and that great hand-fabricated custom air cleaner capping the twin 97s. I wonder what Kilcup's polishing and plating bill was? The coiled fuel and vacuum lines absorb vibration and look really cool. Why don't more people do them that way today? **Bottom**: Twin belts ensure the SCoT pumps out its designated 6 to 8 psi. Reportedly Kilcup made new pulleys after the SCoT-supplied items kept flipping belts. The black flex hose feeds cool air through the custom air cleaner to the twin Strombergs.

Top: Talk about a time warp. Dan Kilcup's neatly-preserved '40 coupe looks for all the world the way it did in '55. The 62-coat Lynton Green lacquer finish hasn't faded a bit.; Dan Kilcup finished his coupe, it's still a looker. **Bottom**: That SCoT-blown motor inspired this author to search for a similar supercharger many years later, and I'm running one on my flathead today. Talk about first impressions.

period leatherette), and the floor and trunk were recarpeted to match. Kilcup added a Stewart-Warner five-gauge instrument panel under the stock dash, (and included a boost gauge, I guess so his wife could track how the SCoT was working!) along with an accessory heater for those chilly Portland winters.

Dan Kilcup initially didn't plan to hop up the painstakingly restored coupe. After all, it was just a commuter for "the little woman." But he'd apparently seen ads for SCoT blowers, and as the engine was out for a "mild rebuild," he really stepped up. A full SCoT kit for a Ford (they came in five sizes, from Crosleys to Cads) when he'd bought the coupe was $362.50. By 1955, when this car was being completed, the flathead was no longer being produced and the blowers may have been discounted.

The superchargers themselves were made in Turin, Italy, and marketed here first under the name Italmeccanica, and later, with a few changes, as SCoT (for Supercharger Company of Turin). Interestingly, the cost of the SCoT alone may have been more than the cost of the entire car, but Kilcup was too committed to stop now.

The 221-ci Ford block was "bored 1/16th inch to Merc," and the stroke was left stock at 3 3/4-inches for a total displacement of 239 inches. He balanced the rods and the Sealed Power split skirt aluminum pistons, and added another expensive item—a Vertex magneto (about $125 in that era—a decent week's wage for a lot of people). Rounding out the modifications, Kilcup fitted a Stewart Warner fuel pump and then he ran up one helluva bill at the chrome platers.

Internally, the engine was cleverly and economically modified to handle the blower's increased punch. The '40 cam was tossed, and Kilcup replaced it with one from a '53 Ford. It probably cost about $35 from a Ford dealer, maybe even less, and it was certainly cheaper than a name-brand cam. I don't recall anyone else doing this. Sukalac reported it was the equivalent of adding "...a semi-race cam with the lugging power of a stock unit." Pretty smart thinking. The ports were mildly cleaned up. Stock Ford valves benefited from stiffer Lincoln Zephyr valve springs; we have to assume he added Johnson adjustable lifters. Everybody did. The oil pressure was reportedly increased, probably with an 8BA pump. Belond Equaflow headers were joined into a single pipe, very likely positioned after twin mufflers. We can only reason this was to keep the car looking rather benign and running quietly considering who it was built for.

According to Kilcup, "...the engine ran like a bomb, for a while." Pressurizing the intake with a supercharger has the effect of increasing the compression ratio. With stock 6.5:1-ratio cylinder heads, the head pressure was simply too high. Kilcup domed out new heads, lowered the c.r. to 5.25:1 and that cured the problem.

The text doesn't mention what sort of rpms Dan turned, but it does say he went through several sets of belts before he machined new blower pulleys. We believe Kilcup was a machinist, possibly professionally, although the article doesn't specify. A close look at his car, built back in the pre-billet era, shows numerous refined updates and hand-built aluminum items that a crack machinist could readily fabricate.

Funny thing is, Mrs. Kilcup apparently never drove "her" coupe. As Sukalac put it, "How did Dan's little woman like the rig? She doesn't get near it. Dan bought her a car of her own. No. She isn't letting him fix this one up."

"Dan Kilcup passed away five or six years ago. He drove the '40 all those years," reports current owner Bob Ames, of Portland, Oregon. "It's an absolutely unchanged survivor." Ames says the little green coupe was well known in the Portland area and among members of the Columbia Timing Association. After Dan's death, one of Ames' friends, Phil Horing, purchased the car—in remarkably well-preserved condition—from Kilcup's estate. He had it a year and then sold it to Steve Webber. Active in the CTA, Webber knew Dan Kilcup. He owned the coupe for four years before selling it to Ames.

The Kilcup '40 "goes like crazy," Ames says. The car now has twin tailpipes, and a Zephyr cluster in a '39 three-speed floor shift gearbox replaces Kilcup's original column shift '40 transmission. Little else has been changed.

Just as we went to press, Ames sold the '40 to well-known Pacific Northwest car collector Gordon Apker. He owns several hot rods, including a '31 Model A highboy roadster with a McCulloch-blown flathead that was featured in the first hot rod class at the Pebble Beach Concours d'Elegance in 1997. Apker is thrilled to have the "time warp" coupe. "It's not going anywhere for a long, long time," he insists. Somehow, I think Dan Kilcup would be pleased. ≈

CHEV-FORD COMB

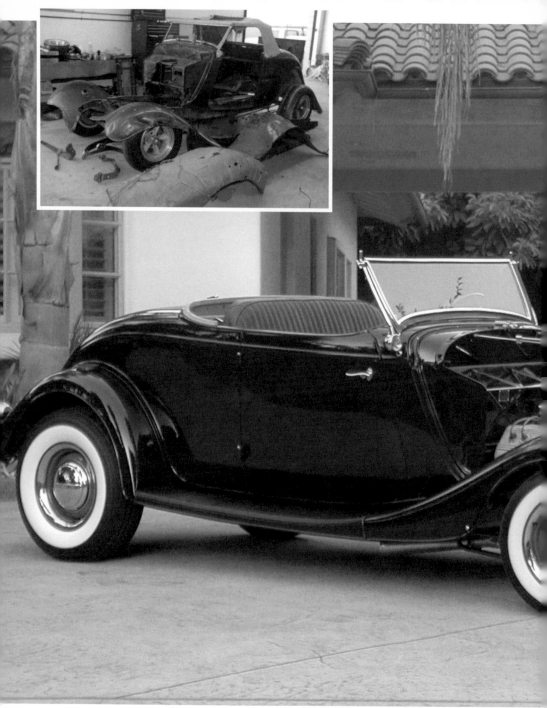

NATION REVISITED

By Drew Hardin

Harry Warner must have loved this '33 roadster. Its story is his story.

He bought it new in Chicago in 1934 and owned it until he passed away in the mid-1990s. The car's current owner, Bill Swanson, tried to buy it from Harry, not once but twice, yet Harry changed his mind each time. It was Harry's son, Dan (who you may know from his involvement with the SCTA and the salt), who sold it to Bill after Harry's passing.

Harry honeymooned in this car with his bride, Helen. He drove it west when he relocated to Los Angeles. But being a Hop Up Guy even back then, Harry couldn't leave the car alone. In 1940 he tore the car apart, buttressed the frame, and installed a Merc flathead, Columbia rearend, Zephyr gears and juice brakes.

Turns out those were just the first of the mods Harry would make to the roadster. In 1947 he acquired the Wayne Manufacturing Company, the six-cylinder speed specialists, and it wasn't long before the Merc was replaced with a Chevy inliner. The ragtop Ford with the mismatched motor became Harry's test mule, home to all sorts of head, cam, and carb setups.

It was in this state that Harry's roadster first appeared in *Hop Up*, in a March 1953 story called "Chev-Ford Combination." Writer Geoffrey Hardin (no relation, I don't think; still out there, Geoffrey?) described the evolution of Harry's car, from the problems he had mating the Chev motor to the Ford trans, to the various carburetor combinations Harry tested before settling on the triple Zenith downdrafts. The exhaust system was trick: From two cast manifolds the exhaust could travel either through a

Those are original Ardun conversions on Bill's 59A Merc flathead. Bill has paperwork that shows the heads were imported from England to North Hollywood in the early Fifties. Ken Austin in Oregon builds custom intake manifolds for Ardun heads. Ken will make one for just about any induction setup, including triple 97s. Vintage Carburetion Technologies set up the Strombergs.

muffled pipe on the left side of the car or through a straight pipe on the right. "From the rear of the car the twin pipes look like any other V-8," Hardin wrote, "but have an entirely different sound." We bet.

For the article, Harry ran the car on a chassis dyno and produced 162 rear-wheel horsepower at 4,500 rpm. Hardin also reported that the roadster turned "90 mph on gas at Pomona." A photo of the car at the SoCal digs—looking bone stock with full fenders—ran with the story.

Bill Swanson told us that Harry used to commute in the roadster from the Wayne shop in Glendale up to his home in the foothills, turning the drive into a test loop. "In fact," said Bill, "there's a guy who came by our shop and told us about racing Harry up Verdugo Road. The guy was in a '55 Corvette and Harry blew his doors off. Can you imagine?" Yeah. The whole idea makes us smile.

When Harry sold the Wayne business, he swapped the inliner for a small-block, and the whereabouts of the potent six are unknown. Although Bill is a Chevy guy (an immaculate, fuel-injected '57 Bel Air and a fuelie '57 Corvette sit in his stable), he didn't want to return Harry's roadster to its inliner incarnation. Instead, Bill wanted to build "a state-of-the-art 1952 hot rod, set up the way Harry would have wanted it."

And so began years of collecting and assembling authentic Ford parts for the roadster's reconstruction. Bill acted as architect of the project, while restorer Art Fernandez built the car. "We're fans of original good stuff," Bill said, so there were scant few aftermarket pieces included in the buildup.

Bill wanted to return the roadster to flathead power and went through a handful of "bad to worse" blocks before finding just the right one: a '48 59A Merc bored 3/8 and fitted with a 1/4-inch-stroked Merc crank. But as the engine was coming along, Bill decided he wanted more than just your everyday flathead (if there is such a thing). Through his network of pals he came up with a pair of original Ardun heads and matched the conversion with a "mild Isky cam, since you don't need much cam with those heads." On top sits a custom intake made by Ken Austin that accepts triple 97s. All the engine work was done by M/V Automotive's Ernie Murashige.

Backing the motor is a transmission much like what Harry was using back in '53: a '39 Ford box filled with 26-tooth Zephyr gears. The '33 Ford axle housing was modified by Eric Vaughn to accept a 3.54:1 ring and pinion. To get the car to sit right, Art mounted a Magnum dropped axle and Pete Eastwood hairpins, reversed the front spring eyes and removed a couple of leaf springs. In back he rebuilt the spring packs and matched them with tube shocks.

Art was amazed to find that the roadster's original wood was still in perfect condition, "and the original undercoat was still in the doors." Art reused the wood and masterfully massaged the metal back into shape (using no plastic, he pointed out). He laid back the windshield posts a bit (which Harry had chopped 2 inches back in '40), and the top was chopped 2 1/2 inches. When the bodywork was complete, Art applied 25 coats of hand-rubbed Washington Blue lacquer, burying forever Harry's Gawd-awful Buick Riviera green paint job.

We photographed the roadster just before it was 100-percent complete. The interior was still a work in progress, but Bill will grasp a '39 Ford banjo wheel and gaze at a custom-made, burl wood instrument panel built by Bob Kennedy and filled with gauges restored by the North Hollywood Speedometer and Clock Company. Bill's backside will rest on sumptuous burgundy leather, stitched in a duplicate of the original pattern.

While Bill and Art are proud of what they've accomplished, they're quick to give credit to Vaughn, Ken Austin, and the other assorted companies and long-time pals who helped them in their quest. "And we've gotta give Harry credit for preserving this car from 1934 to 1994," Bill said.

Yep, Harry Warner must have loved his '33 roadster. We'd bet he'd love it still. 🚗

Top: Harry Warner working on his roadster's inline motor in the early Fifties. Note how Harry had to cut way into the Ford's firewall to accommodate the Chev. **Middle**: Look closely between the bumper and the front fender and you can see the roadster's Magnum dropped axle and modified leaf-spring pack. **Bottom**: The interior is still a work in progress: The burl wood dash and restored instrument panel are in place, but the door panels and upholstery are still to be finished.

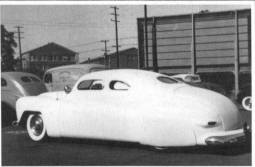

Top: Finished coupe hung in good company, T-roadster; crackerbox boat, etc. **Bottom** (left to right): Business coupe got around in primer condition when it was more acceptable than fashionable. Jack trophied at the Armory Car Show in spite of white-out windows that concealed the unfinished interior!; Stewart is staged at Santa Ana Drags behind another period custom. Earlier, he was present at the first drags at Goleta, but without the coupe.

Roadster Guy's

CUSTOM COLORS

Jack Stewart, co-author of the *LA Roadster Retrospective*, had his Hop Up beginnings as a custom guy. He is NOT the Jack Stewart of "Polynesian" fame, although journalists have made that naive assumption for many years. Our Jack started it all with a '41 Ford business coupe that he street raced for about a year in 1948 before he decided to customize it. He completely removed the front sheet metal to lighten it for the illegal street jousting and put Model A headlights down in front to try to keep it legal. Hardcore. But, hey! That's our Jack.

The first custom touch was a top chop performed at Reg Schlemmer's shop by Kenny Lucas. By now you are beginning to see that Jack was amongst 'em. Some notable names appear here. Next, Jack and a pal channeled the car in his Mom's driveway on a Saturday and drove the thing that night! The next step came not-so-fast. A nine-month stay at the Ayala brother's Auto Butchers netted a new front end fashioned after the new '49 Fords, as well as full fades accomplished with sheet metal. This, Jackson tells us, was the long way but the most correct way to get the deed done. And certainly if our tale is to include everybody who was anybody, then the car went to George Barris for primer and detailing. It was done in one week, just in time for

JACK STEW

George and Jack to take it to Balboa for the Easter Holiday. George himself later painted the car.

It was at this stage that the car went to the Armory Car Show, as seen in the attached pictures, with the windows whited-out to conceal the unfinished interior. A stock, but brute '48 Cad flathead V-8 was in front by this time, and we are told it was a pretty strong runner.

Jack sold the car shortly after the start of the Civil War (actually the Korean War) and relates that since everyone had been drafted, there was no market for hopped-up cars. Their values dropped to nothing, and he got very little for it.

Stewart and East turned the car up in about '72 in a bone yard, they took some photos that they can't find, and now the car is restored and proudly owned by a man named Bob Drake (not that one). It even appeared in *Street Rodder* Magazine lately, where they revisited the 20-year-old article on the restoration. But no mention of Stewart. No problema.

When it comes to promotion, Jack needs no help! 🚗

Top: Current owner/restorer, Bob Drake, poses with the historical custom. **Bottom**: Is this the kid that would drive the girls cuckoo?

HOP UP STYLE BY MAIL ORDER!

NOSE JOB
Weesner nosed roadster
on a banner!
On Graphite
M, L, XL,XXL
$16 + $5 S&H

THE '40
Weesner illustration of our
famous Volume Two cover!
On White
M, L, XL,XXL
$16 + $5 S&H

"en hop up veritas"
BALLCAP
Black with veritas slogan
$15 + $5 S&H

JIVE FIVE
Mayabb rendering of Hop Up
Build Up coupe!
On Black
M, L, XL,XXL
$16 + $5 S&H

TRADITIONAL HOP UP TEE
Same as the original.
Has script on the front
and the logo on the back
M, L, XL,XXL
$16 + $5 S&H

en hopup veritas

"en hop up veritas"
BUMPER STICKER
$3 + $1 S&H

Specify size where necessary and send your scratch to:
HOP UP • PO Box 790 • Riverside, CA 92501

& RAP MUSIC

MISSOURI · 1941
442·143

Ford

They're always sayin,' "The youngsters can't afford our kinda cars these days, Man." Right.

Rustman has had them all: High-tone big-block roadsters, Euro-trash classics, right down to the ultimate '32 Vicky Ratrod. (Ease up, Greasers, it's on the yella license plate.) So when he was trading some iron around with his Pal Wayne, and took in a nice ol' '39 Fo-Do, he knew what to do. He'd Hop It Up. Wreck it for the V-8 Clubbers. Ruin it for life, take away its originality. Right. And give it Hop Up Style while he was at it!

Grab that used trans adapter; bring in the fresh 283 we were gonna use on the whatch-acallit. Get them skirts over there painted black. Take the newspaper off those Olds bumpers we had chromed last year. And call Moser: I need some o' them pricey flippers. And... oh yeah. Lowering blocks. Get a pair of 3-inchers outa that cabinet. That '40 col-umn will go right in and, Hey! Louis just finished rebuilding the '40 trans for the roadster—we'll use that.

And one final trick. They would use scooter fishtails and straight pipes. No mufflers. Let the sucker cackle. Rap. That's Rustman's "Rap Music," played shamelessly at last year's Rattle Can Nationals, over hill and dale, rap on power, rap on compression, and some other threatening note when runnin' steady. It's a scene-stealer. A crowd pleaser. Maybe a little tongue-in-cheek, but definitely a lesson to the economically challenged among us. Find some parts, grab some orphan iron and get out to the shop.

Point is, Amigos Mios, that V-8 four-doors are as cheap as an old car can get. Everybody seemed to be too cool for them

(until now), and you or your poverty-stricken young family man can reasonably fix one up as a tail dragger or hot rod or some combination of the two arts. The formula stated above is just about right, done with parts readily available, 'cept, maybe, the '41 Olds bumpers.

Then you will be—as Rustman says—"Down the Road Motors."

And listenin' to Rap Music.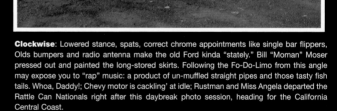

Clockwise: Lowered stance, spats, correct chrome appointments like single bar flippers, Olds bumpers and radio antenna make the old Ford kinda "stately." Bill "Moman" Moser pressed out and painted the long-stored skirts. Following the Fo-Do-Limo from this angle may expose you to "rap" music: a product of un-muffled straight pipes and those tasty fish tails. Whoa, Daddy!; Chevy motor is cackling' at idle; Rustman and Miss Angela departed the Rattle Can Nationals right after this daybreak photo session, heading for the California Central Coast.

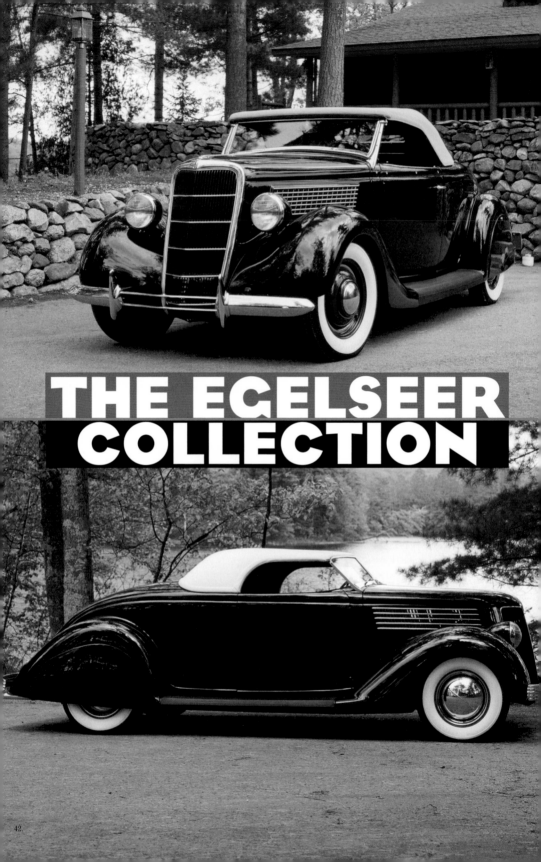

THE EGELSEER
COLLECTION

By Steve Hendrickson

Some guys just never had a chance. Guys like Alan Egelseer, who, as a child in the early '50s, bought his first Model A Ford at age 12. It was about the same time that Alan started noticing magazines like *Hop Up* and *Hot Rod* on the local newsstands. Cars suddenly became more than transportation to him. He was transfixed by those clean, elegant early customs, and by the spare, businesslike hot rods he saw in those pages. His life was changed forever.

That first Model A didn't turn into a hot rod, though. Alan bought it cheap, got it running and looking good, and parked it in his family's front yard, where it easily sold for a tidy profit. More Model A projects followed, and by the time Alan was 16, he had enough money (and enough knowledge, thanks to those magazines) to buy or build whatever he wanted.

A few years later, Alan started what was probably one of the first modern automotive dismantling yards in the country, and that business kept him busy until he sold it a couple of years ago. During that time, he continued messing with cars, but had little time to build them himself. Now that he's retired, though, he's back to hands-on building.

Alan tends towards two kinds of cars: very nice, low-mile originals, and very accurate renditions of early customs and hot rods. These three cars, a '35 Ford roadster, '36 Ford roadster, and '39 Ford convertible, were sharing garage space at his cabin in northern Wisconsin, and they're good examples of the early customs he treasures. As an aside, the other cars hanging around the cabin were a restored '37 Ford roadster (yes, a roadster; so damn rare most folks don't believe in 'em), an original '40 Ford coupe with a hair over 32,000 actual miles on the clock, and a '36 Ford 1/2-ton stake-bed truck, which Alan uses—well, he uses it as a truck, to haul stuff. Even these vehicles aren't all stock though. The '37 roadster had dual exhaust and a pretty snorty sound, the '40 coupe had fender skirts and duals, and the truck sported a just-right rake thanks to big 'n' littles.

THE '35 ROADSTER

Most of Alan's hot rods and customs are built to resemble those done from about 1946 to 1950; this '35 Ford roadster is a bit of a throwback. The idea was to build a car that looked like it was built in about 1940 or '41, by a guy who had Lincoln tastes, but was on a Ford budget. As such, all the parts used are from cars that were style or performance leaders of the time—Lincolns, Auburns and such.

The chassis is restored stock, with the exception of a stock dropped axle; a '40 Ford Columbia 2-speed rearend; de-arched, reversed-eye springs; and '40 Ford juice brakes. The engine is an NOS '41 Mercury 239-ci block, equipped with Eddie Meyer heads and intake, Fenton cast-iron exhaust manifolds, and backed by a '38 Lincoln Zephyr transmission. Note the position of the shift lever in the cockpit. It's ahead and to the left of a Ford.

So far we have a stock looking Ford that's lower and a bit hopped up. The styling changes are what really make the difference. Alan had the windshield chopped 2 inches, and the chopped, folding top was made to resemble a Carson style top, with a French roll along the sides and no seam above the rear window. Under the roof is an interior done in wide-pleated ox-blood leather with wool carpets. Some of the deluxe upgrades include a '39 Lincoln steering wheel, a '33 Auburn dash and gauge panel (with restored Auburn gauges), and a '36 Ford coupe seat. Alan prefers the coupe seat because it hinges up to allow access to behind-the-seat storage.

Dozens of subtle modifications have been made to the car's body, most of which go

unnoticed by all but the faithful. The chrome grille has had its bars painted body color, and a custom bull-nose replaces the stock hood ornament. The stock headlights are lowered 2 inches, and the stock hood sides have an extra set of chrome strips added to each side. Swoopier '37 Ford fender skirts were added by hammer-welding '37 Ford wheel openings into the '35 fenders. The taillights are '35 Ford touring pieces; they're longer, allowing the license plate to be mounted beneath the stalk, and they visually lengthen the fender lines. Bumpers on both ends are Lincoln Zephyr; '38 vintage on the front, and a V-notched '39 in the rear. Stock '35 Ford wire wheels are hidden by Lyon accessory wheel covers, a popular accessory at the time. Ford Sheridan blue paint gives the car a classy, understated look.

This kind of car doesn't happen all by itself, though. Alan is quick to credit Jim Hendricks for the body and chassis fabrica-tion and repair, Doug Lindow for the engine and chassis mechanical work, Sammy Head for the interior, Bill Sturm for the top and side curtains, and Bob Kennedy, who coor-dinated the work in Southern California. The car was completed in 1999 after a five-year build.

THE '36 ROADSTER

This car skips ahead a few years from its older garage mate; Alan wanted this road-ster to recreate that classic custom era that existed right after World War II, when the cars were styled for style's sake, not for points or competition. These cars were built to look good, not win a show; that's an important distinction, one of taste. Alan's inspirations for this car were the customs built by Harry Westergard in that distinct Sacramento style.

In Alan's own words, "Since reading hot rod magazines in the '50s, I've always want-ed to build a custom '36 roadster. In fact, this particular car has been in my head for almost 40 years. In the '60s I bought three '36 roadsters; the first one got restored with minor modifications in the '70s; this one got started in the early '80s but wasn't seriously worked on until the last five years or so.

"The look of the car was always determined to be just the way it is now. The design, blending of various year parts both stock and aftermarket, was set before the project began. The end result is what I always envisioned, with no compromises."

The roadster is based on a stock '36 Ford chassis, fitted with a dropped '40 Ford front axle and sway bar with '40 brakes. The front spring was also de-arched, and the eyes are reversed for added lowness. The steering is also '40 Ford, from the steering box to the column shift and burgundy/black '40 Ford steering wheel. The rearend is a Columbia 2-speed (2.78:1 regular, 2.50:1 in overdrive), with a de-arched spring and '40 Ford hydraulics for stoppers.

Under the hood is a '46 Mercury 59A block with a '49 Merc 4-inch crank, a Potvin Super 3/4-race cam, Eddie Meyer heads and intake, and a pair of Stromberg 97s under that specially made Eddie Meyer air breather. Fenton cast-iron headers feed exhaust to a pair of genuine Smitty steel packs, and behind the motor is a '46 Merc side-shift tranny.

The body is where this car really gets a guy's attention, though. A '36 Ford roadster has great lines to start with, and Alan's restyling job does nothing but improve what Henry started. This is a car that doesn't roll or cruise or drive. It flows. The major modifications include the chopped, Carson-style top and the DuVall windshield; the DuVall makes the car impossibly sleek, and the one-piece top is a small work of art in bare white canvas. The other major elements in making the car work so well are the hood sides, which are stock with added chrome strips, and the '40 Ford fender skirts and

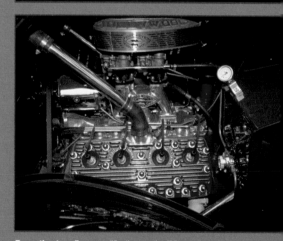

From the top: Every modification on the '35 contributes to the overall illusion without dominating; Auburn dash—complete with instrument cluster—compliments the Lincoln steering wheel; each example is dricen regularly. Alan credites his consortium of contributing craftsmen—we credit the owner as well.

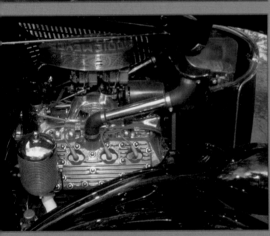

From the top: Each car has clever and tasteful license plate reatment with none on their fronts!; dashboards, instument clusters and trim are also varied and rare; restraint causes appropriate number of doo-dads to appear in the engine compartment.

genuine '37 DeSoto bumpers. The recessed license plate and '39 Ford taillights give it that perfect "Los Angeles, 1949" look.

But if you look close, there are a lot of other little styling tricks on this one. For instance, the headlights have been lowered 2 inches, and the grille sports a new bull-nose strip and a filled crank hole. The cowl is filled and smoothed, the rumble lid has been converted to a trunk and smoothed off, and the spare was moved inside using '40 Ford hardware.

The inside is just as traditional, too. The dash is hand-formed to accept a 1950-vintage Stewart-Warner gauge panel, filled with restored S-W gauges with the genuine early winged logo and curved glass. The front seat is a coupe seat cut down about 6 inches, and everything's covered in dark red leather done in rolls and pleats.

Alan credits Doug Lindow, Sr., with the overall construction and driveline rebuilding; Kent Karlsson with the perfect Carson-style top; Mark Mahood for the paint, Carl Johnson and Terry Hegman for the body work; Dan Krehbiel for the engine and Columbia 2-speed rebuild, Dave Ruesch for the initial construction and restoration, and Bob Kennedy for managing the project and providing encouragement. They did a great job on a great car; just like Alan said. No compromises.

THE '39 CONVERTIBLE

Finally, the youngest of this custom trio, another one that Alan built in that early Westergard/Sam Barris style prevalent in California just after the war. This car started when Alan bought it from Doug Lindow in '89. Doug found the car in the '80s; it was an old custom, already chopped, with no known history. Doug basically restored the car from the top down, then built a Carson-style top to go with the chopped windshield.

Alan loved the car, and eventually talked Doug into selling it. He immediately got to work, making the rest of the car match the sleek roofline. Over time, the car got a lowering job, 15-inch Mercury rims and NOS Cal Custom single-bar flippers, and '40 fender skirts. Later, Alan installed the '37 DeSoto bumpers, had the hood de-chromed and filled, and made a new lower hood "chin" from four original pieces cut and welded together. Other body mods include a '41 Ford gas filler door, a '40 dash to replace the '39, Appleton spots, and a bunch of Offenhauser speed equipment on the car's flathead. In the end, the car ended up being exactly what Alan had in mind, and very close in concept to the '36 roadster. For this one, Alan credits Doug Lindow and Randy Hallman for two rounds of modifications on the car.

And lest you think that any of these are garage queens, Alan reports that the 59A flathead in the '40, built in the '80s, is still running strong after about 40,000 miles. That total includes a couple of cross-country trips, where the Columbia 2-speed helps the car deliver 20 mpg at freeway speeds. This one's as reliable and cool running as it is cool.

It's obvious by looking at the contents of his garage (and what a garage: two levels, with an office that's set up to look like a speed shop) that these cars are not just a passing fancy in Alan's life. Yes, selling used auto parts has made him quite comfortable, and his toy box is bigger than most, but Alan's not a gold-chainer by any stretch of the imagination. He works on his cars, builds them, drives them, and they've been an integral part of his life for more than 40 years. What's more, Alan has a gut feel for what's right on a traditional hot rod or custom, and the cars reflect that in their flawless lacquered sides. When you see one of these cars, either sitting or cruising past, you know inside—maybe not in your gut, but rather in your soul—that what you're seeing is absolutely right. 🚗

From the top: Although each car has its own aesthetic identity, the common theme of period-perfection is clear; '40 dash and column work today for the same reasons as in 1941!; there is no sacrifice to expedience in Alan's cars...generator and accessory parts

MY BLUE HEAVEN

By Peter Vincent

When Ron Sander was a senior in high school, he worked part-time at the Peatzold Body Shop in Portland, Oregon, sanding and taping cars and doing miscellaneous jobs around the shop. Ron had a '48 Chevy Fleetline Aero sedan that he had been customizing, and one day this white '59 Ford Galaxie two-door hardtop appeared in the back of the shop. It sat there for a few days before Ron became curious enough to ask about it. It was a new car with only 3,000 miles on the odometer, and it was in the shop for a complete customizing job. Chuck Atwood of Buhl, Idaho, owned the car and had brought it to be customized at the Peatzold shop.

The '59 Ford spent six months being reworked. After it was finished it was shown throughout the Northwest and garnered many a trophy, including First in Class and People's Choice at the Portland Roadster Show in 1959. It then appeared on the May, 1960 cover of *Rod & Custom* magazine with a full feature treatment inside, which brought the car to national prominence. Original cost for all of this in 1959 was $6000, which was a chunk of change in those days.

Left: Stock side trim and a 4-inch section add to the overall low stance, as does the originally reproduced paint scheme.

Ron lost touch with the car after it left the body shop. Some 31 years later, at a northwest antique car swap meet, he happened to ask someone about the sectioned '59 custom. The fellow he was talking to thought it was stored somewhere in Federal Way, Washington. After following several sources and finally locating the car a year later, he spent two years negotiating with the owner before actually taking possession of the car.

The custom was in very poor condition. It had been sideswiped, poorly repaired, was very rusty and had a fair amount of body rot showing. Ron and Joe Fischer restored the car by replacing all the bad body parts and then essentially redoing all the original bodywork after the car had been media blasted. Ron did the paint work, and Bob Jasper in Tacoma stitched the ivory rolled-and-pleated interior.

When the car had been customized back in 1959, Peatzold took a 4-inch section out of the body. The taillights had been extensively reworked and canted with three '59 Cadillac lenses on each side. A hand-made hood scoop cleared the air cleaner and carburetors on the original engine, which has since been replaced with a 302-inch Ford V-8. The rest of the drivetrain includes a C-4 automatic and a Ford 9-inch rearend. The body had been shaved, but the original side and headlight trim had been left on it. The grille is a Cal Custom tube setup.

What helps keep it all in proportion is the 5-inch lowering job, which was performed on the stock suspension by cutting a couple of coils out of the front springs and using lowering blocks in the rear. The '59 Dodge Lancer hubcaps are in keeping with the originals that were on the car in '59, as are the Coker wide whitewall tires. Ron did a beautiful job keeping the original authentic look with the '55 Dodge Royal Blue metallic paint and scalloped accents, right down to the "My Blue Heaven" moniker. Kudos to you Ron.

From the top: 1959 Dodge Lancer caps and Coker wide whites complete the look; the stock headlight trim was left on; custom formed taillights with three '59 Caddy taillight lenses used on each side.

L.A. ROADSTERS, A RETROSPECTIVE

It's a book that every automotive afficionado will want to complete his library!
It's the all-new "L.A. Roadsters, A Retrospective," a recently released 192-page
volume that traces the history of what is regarded as the nation's most
popular and successful car club, tells how it got started, explains how the
Father's Day L.A. Roadsters Exhibition & Swap Meet came about...and more. Of
interest is the scrapbook format. Publisher Jack Stweart spent more than four
years researching and gathering information on all of the members of the club,
past and present. He got nearly all of them and they are identified, with photos
of their roadsters and other cars, in "L.A. Roadsters, A Retrospective," co-
authored and edited by prominent automotive journalist, Dick Wells.

To order your copy, send a check or money order for $30 (includes $5 for
shipping and handling) to Jack Stewart, 11734 Rives Ave., Downey, CA 90241.
Be sure to include your complete mailing address when ordering.

Order Your Personal Copy Today!

Commercial Collage

We had Thom Taylor reprise some custom trucks last year in *Hop Up* 2001; this time we're looking more at the hard-scrabble hot rod trucks that have always been part of the illusion...the image of a Hop Up Guy at work. A guy that is cool full time—even in the workplace. Granted, most of these heaps won't be haulin' concrete blocks to job sites, but they're sure-nuf trucks that in most cases are a first choice of the owner/builder.

We're way past the time when a guy has to "settle" for something to hop up.

Take a look. Then go find one of those antique truck newsletters, get a restored truck real cheap, and ball it up: slam it, slice it, scallop it, stuff some fire-breathin' V-8 gonads into it, and take it back to the national truck meet for the debut.

A man's gotta have a pickup. Yeah. A Hop Up Truck.

Commercial Collage:
KEITH TUCKER

Photos by Jim Aust

Keith's truck was bought from family friend Bud Goosen. Bud and Keith's own dad, Kenny, had restored the truck in 1961, with the body off, no less. To keep it in the family, Bud recently sold it to Keith, who took certain liberties: a Volare clip to give it IFS, 327 small-block, sagged suspension, and like that. Looks like good work all around!

Commercial Collage:
LYNN BIRD

Photos by Jim Aust

You'll recognize most of what Lynn did to this daily-driven hot rod truck. The top was cut 3 1/2 inches, and that's a Nailhead Buick in there, not some been-there-done-that mill. Using these tricks and more, along with his always perfect eye, Lynn created a sets-right/goes-right truck that's the latest in a heroic line of hot rods from his South Bay garage.

Commercial Collage:
BELL/GRAVES

Photos by Jim Aust

The boys pulled the Planada Truck out of the Moomjeam barn (remember the '32 highboy with the Used Cars lettering all over it?); the '40 Ford running gear had been installed in 1940, from a new wrecked sedan. The paint and lettering happened that year, too. Only evolution from that time is the mild 265 installed in 1955. Fairly avante garde customizing!

Commercial Collage:
MIKE SMITH

'34 Cab, '32 frame, 365 Cad motor, four-speed trans, Olds rear and sounds like the scattered parts a lot of guys own. But do they put them together for a shop truck? Hop Up Guy Mike Smith's Califonia Hot Rods in Sonora, Cal did! On the lower right is pal Scotty Strebl's truck done at the same time. Cool neighborhood, ain't it?

BRAD MILLER

This '41 truck showed evidenc
of a prior life as an Elm
pusher. It had been acquire
through Blair's Speed Sho
(along with a spiced-u
small-block Chevy); and '4
Merc parts complete th
driveline, including the column
shift steering column, trans
rearend and a '40 passenge
car steering wheel.

We can see loving, deliberat
craftsmanship by the owne
in all areas of consideration
But it wasn't enough t
"keep it in the family." Th
toter has given way to
roadster project, facilitate
when a renowned collecto
from Down South took th
suede commercial car awa
from the L.A. Roadster
Show.

Race Cars

Lest you forget: It's about the gow.

Race cars of all kinds prompted backyard, shade-tree novices to focus first on how they ran, and then—and only then—how they looked. So the racers from fairground dirt ovals, Muroc, Bonneville, Daytona, Santa Ana and their counterparts in your part of the country inspired Hop Up Guys to do the deed.

Some old race cars are not practical to use anymore and—if ever there was one—they are an example of rolling sculpture: a rare incident of past-functional-art-reposing. We may let ya get away with not running one of these.

Turn the page and as we say so often: You're just gonna have to imagine the sounds.

Stand on it and turn left. Or not. They might just be ol' drag monsters, too!

RODDERS GO R

By Jim Chini

With the onset of World War II, the government mandated a halt to all motorsport competition in the United States. The ban took effect on August 1, 1942 and would remain until September 1945. Hot rodders, being a resourceful group, were not deterred by this restriction. Through frugal use of gasoline and tire rationing stamps, a few of those who were not in military service managed to stage a handful of "secret" (and technically illegal) lakes meets during this period.

By mid-1945, government enforcement of the ban had become lax, and oval races for the roadsters began to be openly held in San Bernardino on a track called the Gate City Speedway. This venue was literally nothing more than a plowed field. There were no grandstands and only a snow fence for a crash wall. Nicknamed the "Ash-Can Derby," this primitive beginning would blossom over the next two years into a coast-to-coast oval track phenomenon known as the "Roaring Roadsters."

The star of these Ash-Can Derby races was a lanky 15-year-old named Troy Ruttman who, in 1952, became the youngest-ever winner of the Indianapolis 500. Half of that year's starting line-up was comprised of former track roadster drivers, including second-place finisher Jim Rathmann (who would win the event in 1960).

While Southern California was the hot bed of roadster racing, highly competitive circuits developed in the San Francisco Bay Area, the Pacific Northwest, Arizona, Chicago (under the management of the Granatelli brothers), and the Indiana/Ohio

Photo by Russ Reed

Photo by Ernie Lovingood

Top: The "Big Three" of post-war roadster racing in Southern California—left to right: Troy Ruttman, Manuel Ayulo and Jack McGrath. They became three of the most feared competitors at Indianapolis and on the AAA National Championship trail in the 1950s. The photo was taken in early 1947 at the Bonelli Stadium in Saugus, California, which was at that time the "home track" for the California Roadster Association. All three cars had Ford V-8 power under the hoods. **Left**: Pat O'Connor honed his skills on the tough Mutual Racing Association circuit in Indiana and Ohio. He won three championships on the AAA/USAC Midwest sprint car circuit, and in 1953 (shown here) made his first attempt to qualify for the Indy 500. His beautiful Gordon Schroeder-built Brown Motor Company Offenhauser was too slow by less than 1 mph! Over the following five years he would be a heavy favorite to win the race, taking the pole position in 1957. On the first lap of the 1958 race he died in a tragic multi-car accident.

Photo by Russ Reed

area. These circuits not only produced a large number of drivers that would dominate American oval track racing well into the 1960s, but also an almost endless list of mechanics, fabricators and accessory manufacturers. Companies like Ansen, Edelbrock, Grancor and Hilborn rose to international prominence during this period.

Of all the mechanics and fabricators, probably none enjoyed the level of fame and success that the legendary A.J. Watson did. In addition to being the chief mechanic for four Indianapolis 500 winners, Watson's Glendale, California shop produced seven winning cars. In 1963, almost half of the starting line-up consisted of Watson-built cars.

Sadly, by 1957 track roadster racing had all but ceased to exist, felled by a combination of circumstances over which the sport had no control. Among these factors were

Opposite page, from the top: In 1947, Pat Flaherty took leave of his Glendale, California home and the Southern California track roadster circuits. Along with the Ruttman brothers, Jim and Dick, he moved to Chicago and became a headliner on the Granatelli brothers' Hurricane Hot Rod Association circuit, which had Soldier Field as its home track. Pat qualified for his first Indianapolis 500 in 1950 driving this Kurtis-Kraft 3000 that was partially owned by Andy Granatelli and sponsored by Grancor Automotive. In 1956, Pat teamed up with his old Glendale roadster racing pal A.J. Watson to win the 500. He still lives in Chicago but has replaced his racing passion with pigeons; Bob Sweikert roared out of Northern California's track roadster ranks to win the Indianapolis 500, the National Driving championship, and the Midwest sprint-car title in 1955—a triple that has never been duplicated. In 1950, on the high-banked Oakland Stadium half-mile track, he drove this beautiful sprint car, owned by lakes legend Karl Orr, to a then-world-record speed for "stock blocks" of over 115 mph. Orr had a fuel-injected Mercury V-8 under the hood. **This page**: The first all "hot rodder" assault on the Indianapolis 500 came in 1950 with this machine bankrolled by lakes-competitor-turned-auto-dealer Bob Estes, built and wrenched by Jud Phillips, and driven by California Roadster Association star Joe James. The car had a potent Ardun-Ford under the hood, but it just wasn't enough to make the field against the sophisticated Offenhausers.

Photo by C.V. Haschell

From the top: One of the greatest race car drivers in American history, the legendary Jim Bryan got his start on the rough-and-tumble post-war Arizona track roadster circuit. From the fall of 1953 through his win at Indianapolis in 1958, Bryan totally dominated American National Championship racing, winning three championships and more than one-third of all races contested by Championship cars. Bryan was equally proficient in midgets and, as shown here in this 1952 photo from Terre Haute, Indiana, the ever treacherous sprint cars; Chuck Hulse, whose brother Ed was the cover boy of the very first issue of *Hot Rod* magazine, was a mainstay of the California Roadster (and later Racing) Association for almost 10 years. He later moved on to the United States Auto Club, participating in all of its open-wheel divisions and in the Indianapolis 500. This 1959 photo shows Chuck in the famed Morales Brothers "Tamale Wagon," which carried him to the CRA title that year. The car was built by Tucson roadster graduate Roger McClusky, who became one of USAC's major stars, winning five championships in three different divisions.

the fickle taste of the racing fans, who gravitated toward the burgeoning late-model stock cars, and an ever-increasing shortage of the primary base of a track roadster— Henry Ford's 1925 - '27 Model T. Most significant, however, were Wally Parks and his newly formed National Hot Rod Association. For every track roadster driver there were probably 100 youngsters who longed to race but lacked the funds and/or the talent necessary to compete on an oval track.

Parks and his NHRA legitimized quarter-mile drag racing and provided safe, well-supervised venues for these young men to get the racing bug out of (or in many cases, deeper into) their systems. Along with the competitors came the fans, and the "Roaring Roadsters" became a distant but very significant piece of American auto racing history.

As a footnote to history, in the mid-1980s, when the revitalized street rod industry made repro roadster bodies as easy to get as a Big Mac, a group in Tucson, Arizona tried to resurrect track roadster racing. This comeback lasted barely two seasons.

Eddie Bosio
BEEN THERE, DONE THAT
STILL DOIN' IT!

Coot? No Way.

So Rustman says, "'Know who Eddie Bosio is?"

"Yeah, won Oakland in the Fifties with the roadster he bought from Edelbrock."

"Yeah, and he built a clone of it a few years ago. And he's 84 and buildin' another highboy now. Wanna go see him?"

Sign my ass up!

It became a pilgrimage for the River City Roadsters. We'd fly to Sacto, they'd pick us up in a couple of roadsters, we'd blaze a hundred miles or so and meet this coot.

Coot? No way. Eddie Bosio is the youngest 84 we have ever met. Why is that a recurring theme with hot rod types we meet? It must be good for us, hmmmm?

Eddie's story begins about a half-generation before most of the lakes guys we read about. He was interested in dirt oval racing in the mid-to-late Thirties, got a ride because he GAVE the car to a guy to make race car, then, after proving some merit as a chauffer, better cars were offered to him. We particularly like the black '29 in the accompanying photos. It was owned by Freddie Demartini and Tommy Skahill, ran pretty good and had the look. It must have evolved from a street hot rod because the shell is filled, shortened (look at the nice grille), it sits about right, and man, is it set up flat on that turn or what?!

For some reason or another, Eddie got distracted from racing, bought the Vic Edelbrock Sr. roadster and began to act on some innate feelings about how things should look; about how things should be

Top: Eddie sets up the A-V8 for the turn; **Bottom** (left to right): Push car appears to have Hop Up Credentials, too; Ex-Edelbrock Roadster won Oakland, and merited professional model on Southard-shoot.

done while making them look better. That bent for fine style and build quality resulted in the '56 Oakland Roadster Show America's Most Beautiful Roadster prize. Over the years the car was subtly changed and it eventually went away. We think somebody knows what it ultimately became. Maybe some modified every-day street rod or something.

But Eddie moved on and on, most recently with an in-liner motivated, four-speed '55 Chevy hardtop. He took the four of us for a ride in it and, Boys, it stops as good as it goes! Believe it. The car is beautifully turned-out, detailed to the bone (has Greek-style dollops on it) and, Gawd!

This is a cool guy.

The new roadster is a Wescott-bodied, Chevy-powered piece that exhibits the detail (frenched Pontiac taillights, clever switching to open trunk, detail, detail, detail) that this cat has always employed. Its main occupation will be to transport Eddie and his lady to tie up with life-long pal Fresno Jake ('34 highboy) and cruise the foothills of the Sierra Nevada 'til the roads run out.

Don't guess we hafta tell Eddie Bosio to grab a gear, now, do we? 🚗

From the top: The Oakland Roadster Show winner was a street warrior, seen at all the Bay Area outings of the day; personalized nerf is one of the trademarks of Eddie's gang of Valley Rodders; the Chevy hardtop.

PATINA
PERSONIFIED

SPURGEON-GIOVANINE
LAKESTER
IS FOUND!

Patina. It's become trite lately. Everything that is old and half worn-out is patinaed. The dictionary has a more narrow take on it, citing old bronze and the greenish rust that happens there.

In our colloquial rod-speak, that word can sometimes translate to turd. Oh yeah. If it's a turd you call it "patinaed" and we all get fuzzy and love it.

The Spurgeon-Giovanine Chevy roadster would be a piece o' poop if it were an unidentifiable relic, but we know from whence came this little race car. It was only about 10 years old when young guys started cutting on it, then had about 25 years of glory before it reposed in the high desert for almost 30 more.

Along came David Lawrence who, with a sign written on a napkin, "Old race car wanted," met the car's owner at the time. The guy took him to the high desert and David brought home his race car. And began to study.

The new custodian found that the car, a 1925 Chevy roadster, had run the lakes and Bonneville, originally with the correct hopped up '25 Chevy running gear, enhanced by an Olds three-port head and 3:27 Model A gears in the Chevy rearend. It was run by Spurgeon and Giovanine (the same Giovanine who recently passed and whose similar four-banger roadster still runs at the same venues). This, and future iterations of the car, was documented in *Hot Rod* Magazine. Its evolution through a Jimmy motor and eventually to the Jimmy in the rear (mid?) is well documented, along with the physical evidence of its last attempted incarnation to a drag-race rig, never completed.

Karl Borgh ran the car in '54, '55 and '56 as the "Mothersills Special," and it is said that during this time, at a party, a reputedly drunken Von Dutch striped this and another car. No stripes remain on the carcass today, but they look like Von Dutch work in HRM feature photos from the Borgh era.

After Lawrence got it, the car made a run through a high tone auction—as is—but did not create the envisioned bidding war. "Fine. We'll do it ourselves." The obligatory restoration has begun with parts accumulating (hoarders note: David needs virtually everything hardware-wise) and interviews with candidate craftsmen.

This project, when completed, will be part of a "Dream Team" of race cars in the owner's mind: Spurgeon-Giovanine, belly-tank, streamliner.

RYAN SPE[
DAD'S CAR 50 Y

Father's Day 2001. No, this isn't coverage of the big roadster meet. This is a tale about one of our favorite subjects. Three generations (you'll see it elsewhere in *Hop Up* 2002) of car guys—Gramps, Junior, and III—all gear heads, doin' the deed. Bein' cool. Wrenchin.' Diggin' old iron.

Did you know IT'S ABOUT THE IRON? Oh yeah.

Minnesota Hop Up Guy Bob Ryan is the Junior. In our rants back and forth over the last year he has spoken less about his own projects than "Dad's" coupe. Dad had run a "stocker" in Minnesota Stock Car Racing Association races in South Dakota, Minnesota and Wisconsin, in 1950, 1951, 1952, before he went to Korea. The "stocker" handle on the cars meant they had to look stock outside and even under the hood, so in-the-innards is where you tried to make a difference.

Senior's '32 3-window coupe ran a '48 59L block, 3 $\frac{3}{8}$ x 4, one stock carb, a truck

rearend with floating axles, some suspension tweak in the way of sway control front and back, and full fenders. Yup, had to look 100-percent stock! (Wonder how many Ford fenders went away that way?) The unseen Ryan touch must have been effective because, in 1951, he won the State Fair Championship. Last year was the 50th anniversary of that accomplishment, so Senior began to think about a commemorative car. Junior came up with a nice donor, turned it over to his Dad, and then watched.

"It was Dad's deal. He ran the project; we just stood back and watched."

Opposite page, from the top: All the action shots we saw had 3020 in the lead. 1951 State Fair Championship was the result; Bob Ryan Sr. is project manager and crew chief on the "Ryan Special" commemorative car; Some other Ryan Racing doo-dads show up in this photo.

This page, from the top: 3020 is the street address of the Bee Line Alignment shop that sponsored the coupe; coupe runs the streets today with open headers. All Ryan projects include nice "Appointments."

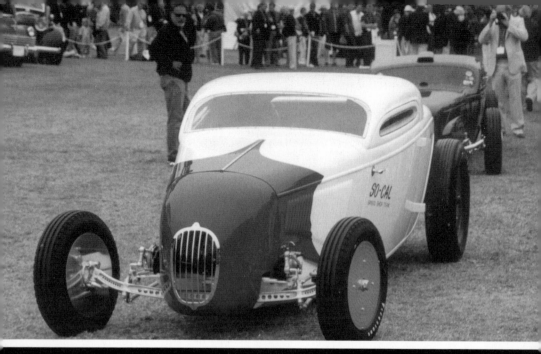

Grass

It's not a personality contest.

It's the ultimate hot rod show. And although we don't hang too much in the show set, at least at Pebble Beach the rod and custom element allowed on the green is traditional.

Always Hop Up Style.

So when last year's competition coupe class laid out the top three in some apparent order, we were not vested in the results: Hop Up Guys won all three places. The Chrisman/Duncan/McPherson, Pearson/Meyer, and So-Cal/Orosco cars could have been presented in any order and we'd-a been toastin' the whole deal. They're all pals of ours; they are among the best rod builders, restorers, collectors and caretakers in motorsport and, Hey! They're kin.

But only one can win first place and it was DBO—Don Orosco and his team—for the So-Cal Coupe. Well frickin' done, Boys. We suggested as much in our Hop Up Volume II coverage of the restoration project, but Goodgawdomighty! These guys go all the way, and it's not just about money. Correctness drives them to extremes that may not be met in classic car restoration. Ya see, there's elements about the evolution of a hot rod racecar that make picking a moment in time...interviewing the guys who did the bubble gum welding...finding out who gave what manifold to the car for use with which motor...and, you know...dozens of forensic issues have to be satisfied, and then thoughtful and skilled execution of craft have gotta be employed to end up here.

Has a golf course ever seen such bad-ass race cars? Not bloody likely. **Top of the page**: Two views of Don Orosco's stunning So-Cal Coupe, which bested two other stunning coupes on the green at Pebble; the DBO Motor Racing crew responsible for the restoration include (from left): painter Mike Sanchez, chief fabricator Olle Eriksson, crew chief Brad Hand and painter Che Burns. **Bottom of the page**: Don Orosco's So-Cal crew turned out for the concours in faithful reproductions of the 1953 Glendale Sidewinders team jackets, accessorized by white pith helmets straight outta Bonneville; how do you pick just one to win?; original So-Cal team owner Alex Xydias jives with Orosco, while Hand looks on; Bruce Meyer and Pete Chapouris with the Pierson Brother's coupe copped second in a tough room; another DBO group shot, this time with Orosco and his son, Patrick; three combatants and close friends— Don Orosco, Art Chrisman and Bruce Meyer—pose in front of Chrisman's coupe.

Hop Up Style

Yeah, Daddy. It's Hop Up Style and it comes in all kinds of packages.

Fifty years ago it might have been crackerbox boats. Cycle races on Catalina Island, or Lake Elsinore. Maybe a hard look at the new Indy Roadster by Kurtis, or an innovative new roadster based on something foreign.

Today you cats are as cool, but you're better. Ya see, Hop Up Guys have the advantage of the recorded shenanigans of those who preceded us, we have knowledge of the evolution of rod and custom fashion (something we generally reject), and we have our own familiarity with cool.

What we got here, Ol' Comrade, is an eclectic bunch of personalities, collections, a car or a motorcycle, a one-owner hot rod from the Forties...Hell, Man, they're the '02 happenings of hot rod guys and chicks who are the definitive, the benchmark, the touchstone, the pulse of cool.

Hop Up Style.
Say it.

Somewhere West of Laramie... and East of Santa Monica...

Personality profile? Car collection feature? Shop visit? Interview with long-time racer? Our recent visit with Harold Johansen was all this and so much more that we can hardly establish a starting reference point. So we will ramble:

NOT related to, but often confused with Howard Johansen, Harold was about 15 years old and happened by a police impound lot on his way home from school. Noticing a Model A roadster with missing fenders, the aspiring gearhead went on the snoop and found the car was blessed with a two-port Riley setup on the A motor.

"Hey!" A mature voice barked behind him. "You wanna buy the car?"

"How much?"

"Storage on it is $29.75."

Harold hurried home and borrowed the money from his Dad. Cool Dad, huh?

Well, that swindle was the beginning of an internal combustion tango that continues today, still includes that very Model A roadster (the centerpiece of one of the nicest collections of Fords we have had the pleasure to inspect), and initiated a motorsport avocation and racing career the likes of which will probably never be matched.

He began racing the A at the lakes, moved to a T roadster with a rare Riley V-8 overhead conversion, and had a fling at the drags. (Saugus, where Lou Baney ran him off for running a 3/8 x 3/8 motor with stock heads so he could run in the stock class!) But he always found the greatest satisfaction

From the top: portrait of a guy and his first car—50 years later!; Model '40 is a low-low mileage original; this oughta be the Hop Up road show truck.

racing at the lakes and Bonneville. And race he does: Harold held the D Gas Roadster class record for 22 years. Ya gotta be good for your records to stand that long. He recently held the C Gas Roadster record at 208. He got in the Two's in 1975, and today tends to trade Vintage Four records with fellow fireman Roy Creel.

Of course, this is some interesting company for Hop Up Guys with an idea to race flathead fours. Harold is building a flathead motor that will probably go 120. Looks like we just met the first member of the Hop Up 100 Mile Per Hour Club! This motor will run three 97s (or two Webers) and will give us novices something to dream about. There is another interesting banger in the engine shop. This one is an aluminum "D" block that will get a Rutherford rocker arm head. It keeps company with flathead V-8s, of course, the occasional SBC, and A and B blocks in abundance, reflecting job security for the engine shop and future racing efforts.

The machine room has the obligatory Bridgeport mill, huge lathe, and all machine work but crank grinding is done "in house."

The car collection is heavy in bangers, shows nothing newer than a Model 40, and there are no "projects" there. These are all completed cars (or remarkable originals), with one or two getting engines redone, but otherwise complete and restored.

A Close List Looks Like This:

The original 1929 roadster (two-port Riley)

Another 1929 roadster (four-port Riley)

Perfect 1927 roadster body (unattached)

1933 pickup (Cragar)

BB truck (SBC) Gets Bonneville duty some years

1932 Panel truck (Cragar)

1932 3-window coupe (Cragar)

1934 roadster (V-8 flathead)

1933 tudor (under 40K mile original)

1929 coupe (Winfield flathead) Goes to B-ville some years w/ 3.27 gear.

1932 roadster (motor out)

1932 roadster (perfect, maybe nicest Mr. Johansen's seen)

1932 5-window coupe (motor out)

1934 pickup (motor out)

1927 track nose roadster (Offenhauser) Yeah, Offy!

From the top: Ford guys go on sensory overload in rooms like this. As, Bs, Model 40's. Nothing later or earlier; Harold tweaks on an overhead banger conversion of his own design/manufacture one off. Don't ask; oh, and about that genuine timing tag you paid $65 for?

And then there's the successful race car, Number 32. Steel A body, rare today among mostly glass A bodies on competition cars.

So *Hop Up* has a new best friend. Racer, restorer, collector, machinist, engineer, he's another sage from whom to pry speed secrets and tales of "the day"; another role model among the hot rod guys and gals that make up this crazy quilt of Hop Up personalities. Harold fits in chronological order with the earliest names in hot rod performance, as well as the next generation, and the next, and...that makes sense when you figure that he has literally raced in seven decades, a record that may not have been beaten by any one yet.

We're not feelin' so cocky about that Vintage Four

From the top: This is not your typical scrap iron pile. Harold is likely to emply most of it in one way or another; it seems every raised hood revealed a gem, like this Offy in a track-nose roadster; one of several running Cragar "jigglers" in the collection.

Top: Motto: "No wasted parts"—results in austere, purposeful look. Shotgun exhaust is by owner. **Bottom**: Flanders drag bars, stock tank, '40 Ford mirror, oil tank, battery and coil are all subtly relocated for function and form.

OBBER

: UP HIS CYCLE ROOTS

Hop Up was notorious for showcasing style and performance. That style could be found in less obvious places like crackerbox boat racing, motorcycles in Elsinore, and certain-sure: rods and customs.

In our travels, the broad scope of Hop Up Style is no better or more broadly found than in the shop of Peter Eastwood. P. Wood. Prince Pete. The other Pete. We pretty regularly boast about him on the web page because he is founded in so damned many areas of our own interest and he probably is in fact responsible for our expanding interest in some fairly obtuse areas due mainly to his enthusiasm and intellect. More on all that on another mission.

It's not a surprise, then, to find a motorcycle (motocycle) in the shop, since Indians and Harleys, the occasional Aerial, and who knows what else have been in there from time to time. The key is that these examples are virtually always his own. Granted, they typically find their way into other guys' collections, but during the process, they are Pete's. It's easier that way. There's no customer budget to fret about; there is no attempt at "artistic collaboration," we'll call it. What we'll get here is a pure effort, conceived by and executed by the same artisan.

And what we will find here is simplicity. There will be no sacrifice to the gods of evolved style. Not that. The no-frills approach. Where unexcelled visual joins with no-nonsense practicality, blended into a whole that defies modernists to figger out how the damn hell he did that. It's so simple and it works so good!

That's just P. Wood, Boys.

This is one in a long line of custom Sportsters, but the first with a rigid frame. It's a 1973 that had a street-type restoration about 15 years ago and was going to complement Pete's policy of using every lovin' thing there that is useable ("no wasted

parts") and to create no monuments to his ability to buy things or to his ability to redesign something that doesn't need redesigning. Not a bad lesson for rodders and customizers, too, huh?

You will see the odd something-less-than-chauvinistic gesture of respect for tradition: It took some real shopping to find the Dunlop K70 rear tire. Although in production, and certainly the right choice for this scooter, you can't find them at the Harley accessory stores because they're too narrow. Oh yeah. Cats today want to see if they can make their Harleys look like a Ninja. (Let's spend a bunch of money on THAT!)

So, Eastwood's California Bobber is a product of artistic vision. It demonstrates creative restraint, fabrication skills employed toward performance and customization, and symbolizes the "whole" that is Hop Up Style. If we can't explain it, well, we can feel it. It is in our gut, once our eyes and ears and hands deliver their messages to our noggin.

We got it good, Boys. 🚗

Top: Note 40° raked neck, and stock front fork with non-essentials removed. Both front and rear hubs are black enamel with stainless spokes. **Bottom**: Rear view features N.O.S. Bates fender with manufacturer's paint still on it.

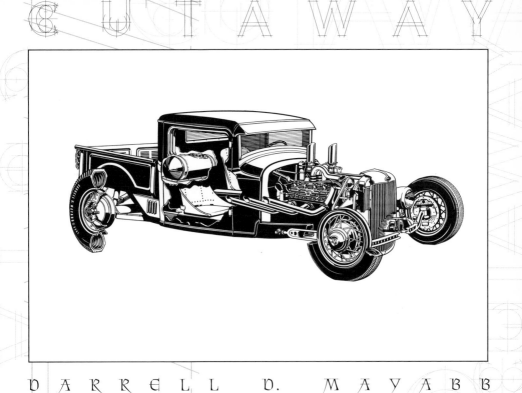

DARRELL D. MAYABB
© 2 0 0 1

One way, in the past, we viewed a
Hot Rod was the CUTAWAY.
Jimmy Shine's '34 Hot Rod Pickup is a great
example of the craftsmanship a modern builder
can bring to a long standing idea of
the modified automobile.
A Cutaway Print is available of
this beautifully crafted Hot Rod.

$ 20   unsigned print 17" x 11"
$ 30   signed print 17" x 11"
$ 50   Lt. Edition print 17" x 11"
          (signed and numbered by the artist)
$ 6.50 shipping

AUTOMOTIVE GRAFFITI 10180 WEST 73RD PLACE, ARVADA, COLORADO 80005-3878
1-303-420-7200

HOP UP HOW TO

Traditional Is Cool...
Safe & Traditional
Is Way Cool!

By Mike Bishop

O ne of the best things about the resurgence of the hot-rod movement is the return to basics: simple, elegant solutions hand-crafted by owner-builders and their pals, the way it was most often done in the day. A big difference, however, is that the tool arsenal today is a whole lot bigger and better than it was back then, which just makes rod building all the better, or so you'd think.

Truth to tell, some of the folks today are carrying on a piece of the tradition that many of us white-headed galoots and graybeards would just as soon forget. It's a romanticized vision, with the way things were in the day seen as a time when young guys cobbled together crude road rockets of awesome horsepower and drove to hell and back looking for excitement.

There's a bit of truth in that image. For sure, some did cobble together crude rides, but they were hardly road rockets. Awesome horsepower existed only in the imagination of most, and as for driving to hell and back . . . well, we were tickled if we could get as far as the little burgs just 50-60 miles north and south of our own little burg and then home again. Certainly that was the case with many of my pals and me in our early hot-rodding years, when we were penniless high-school teenagers.

Not only were many of us short on the long-green, we were also shy of much of the good fundamental info needed to build strong, safe, and otherwise bitchin, hot

Above: This Keith Tardel-built roadster pickup has it all, including new-car reliability resulting from expert fabrication and 100-percent rebuild of all mechanicals—engine, transmission, rearend, brakes, steering —before it hit the road. With 20K-plus trouble-free miles on the odo it's just as solid as it was when it first turned a wheel. **Left**: This is a textbook example of what can be done with a MIG welder and zero knowledge and experience. Called "bubblegum" for obvious reasons, it's the result of power and wire-feed settings that are much too low. Gotta wonder if the guy even noticed the perfect stitching of the spring eye to the bracket on the purchased part and why his work didn't look that good.

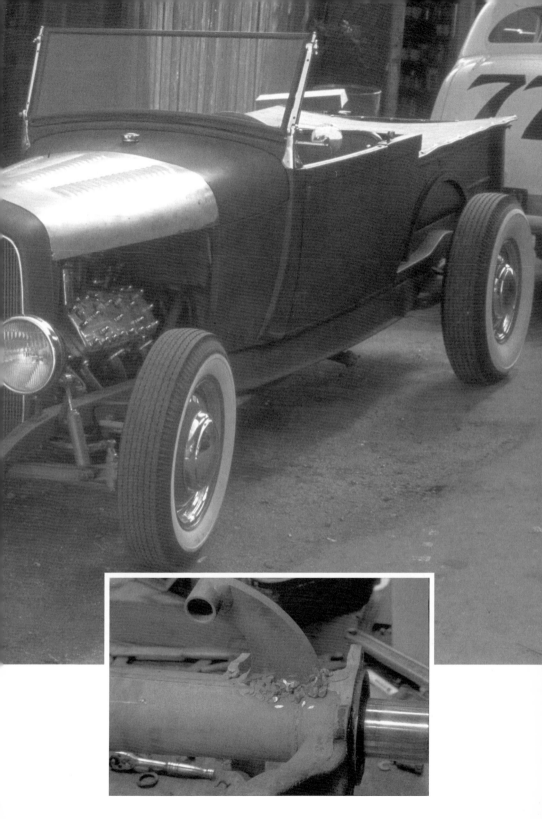

This rough old rascal from the day has a decent presence—good stance, nice balance, many correct details—and crude but strong workmanship.

rods. Each month we would suck all of the high-zoot goodness out of the go-fast articles in *Hot Rod* magazine and then argue among ourselves about the latest hot setup. Never mind that we could neither afford the hardware involved nor did we have the tools or skills to carry out anything more complicated than basic routine maintenance. And that was the last thing we were interested in. Most of us were into the idea of hot rodding almost to the exclusion of acquiring basic car-care skills. Where was the excitement in servicing wheel bearings or doing a brake job?

In those early years, frequent simple breakdowns and no-starts were part of the day-to-day hot-rodding experience. It was the catastrophic failures that earned our full attention and were featured in our burger-stop tales. They were events like a rear wheel and tire combo liberated to wander into oncoming traffic when an axle end had finally taken all the abuse it could stand. Or maybe it was a grenaded transmission that left an embarrassing mess of Sta-Lube and

shrapnel in the high-school parking lot. And jeez, don't forget that grille-destroying rear-ender that resulted when there wasn't enough time to double-pump some pedal pressure back into a very tired set of Henry brakes.

Most of us eventually learned and began to apply the fundamentals of the less-glamorous aspects of hot rodding. The funny thing was, doing the ho-hum work actually made the hot-rod stuff all the better. It allowed us to spend our energy on finding out how to go quick and fast and not just how to get home.

So, with all that's known and all the super tools available today, I'm at a loss to understand why there are still some scary piece-of-junk hot rods being built and driven, with little benefit from sorting out or on-going improvement. It doesn't appear to be a poorboy thing; not a lot of high-schoolers are building these cars. Some badly built rods show up at spendy events, a long way from home, and often with pricey accommodations and lots of suds and sustenance involved, so it's not a shortage of funds that's dictating shabby construction.

While there are probably some conscious and intentional bad-boy plots being played out here—live fast, die young, leave a mangled corpse—my guess is that it's mostly an absence of good info and help in acquiring the skills needed to build safe as well as cool. There's no reason for remaining skill-deprived, however. Read, ask, learn, practice, and do.

More than anything else, affordable high-tech MIG and TIG welders have revolutionized the home-built car hobby overall, and have brought a special blessing to hot rodding in particular. To understand the extent of the blessing, compare the agricultural-like stick welding that was the standard in hot rodding 50 years ago with the precise beads that are routine today. For all that, however, modern welders have bestowed a curse on the movement by giving undertrained rodders a false sense of their ability to correctly stick metal together. Modern welders aren't magic. Just like the old stuff, they require good information and practice on the part of the operator to produce strong welds.

One of the better sources for gaining skill with fitting and welding is a friend or acquaintance who already possesses the skills you're looking for. A well-meaning pal with just a few hours of torch time with a 110 pocket MIG isn't going to be much help here, unless you're interested in stitching nothing thicker than sheetmetal and are up for a lot of trial and error education. Look for the guy with the pro skills and pay attention to what he tells you, including recommendations for buying a welder when you're ready.

Lacking someone to lead you by the hand, you can find excellent training in the night-school voc-ed programs at most community colleges. If that's not an option, buy a good welding textbook, like *Welding Skills and Practices* by Joseph Giachino and William Weeks (about 20 bucks). This one's as good

With the bubblegum ground away, followed by some chamfering with a die grinder, the joints on this axle housing were welded correctly. All that was missing the first time around was good information. And practice.

The thin-wall tie-rod end was not intended for duty as the end of a rear radius rod where it's subjected to high shear loads. The fellow might have gotten by with this modification if the tie-rod end had been sunk most of the way into the radius rod before it was welded in position.

The inelegant details of this 50-year-old frontend are a product of the tools available at the time: hacksaws, hand files, and stick welders. The car is smartly built and super tough, nonetheless.

Above: Contrast the results obtained on this shock/headlight mount with common present-day tools—a plasma cutter, MIG welder, and hand-held high-speed grinders—to the equivalent work of 50 years ago. Strong looks a lot better today. **Right**: Seen from underneath, this extensively modded Deuce crossmember will accommodate a five-speed Tremec as well as anchor the front wishbone and rear radius rods in a GEMSA-head, four-banger-powered 5-window highboy. It's as tough as it is crafty.

as it gets, covering all welding mediums and techniques, plus it's a major source of correct metal fitting information.

You don't have to get all the way into heavy fabrication and welding to rile the safety and reliability gremlins, of course. They've been festering in old car parts as far back as the day and then some. Best thing to do is don't give 'em the opportunity to spoil the fun. At the very least, start with sound mechanicals —brakes, steering, suspension, and drivetrain. Everything doesn't have to be totally fresh, as long as it's all within original service specs. Although there's a special, kinda spiritual connection to one's gearheadedness that comes from driving a 50, 60-year-old car that's mechanically brand new!

There's lots of good stuff to be found in major components harvested from old restos that are being street rodded. The secret here is to educate yourself about the hardware you seek. Get to know what's good, what needs rebuilding, and become comfortable with the work required to bring those old pieces to as-new condition. This is

core information about the very car you're building, information that will serve you well in keeping the car in first-rate shape and provide you with essential insights when things go awry, as they invariably do in old machines.

If you're working with traditional chassis schemes, pay attention to the original suspension plot and how it works, and don't stray so far with your modifications that you induce unwanted problems. When you're making significant changes, like splitting a wishbone or relocating a steering box, think about the part or assembly being modified or moved around: what it does, how it does it, and how your modifications will affect its purpose and the way it functions.

And be realistic in assessing your car-building skills and capability. Few of us have all the tools we think we need, and many of us are not as proficient at operating the complex ones as we would like to be. That's what pals are for, and why hot rodding has always been such a social thing. ⚙

DAD'S TALL T

By Aaron Kahan

To the untrained eye, my dad's '24 T coupe appears to be a real old timey "Tin Lizzie." Some might call it a resto rod, but it was built way before that term existed. Alan Kahan's hot rod may appear a bit stock, but that was the goal. The idea was to build a bit of a sleeper: true to the characteristics of a stock T, while able to stand on its own as a souped-up hot rod.

Dad's interest in cars came from his father, Ben, who worked for his father disassembling cars for their junk recycling business. When my dad was growing up, Ben pointed out unusual cars and taught him how to identify them. But it wasn't until the summer of '55 that my dad became obsessed with hot rods. As a 15-year-old student at Van Nuys High he quickly took note of what his peers were driving. One kid had two Olds-powered hot rods, a T-bucket and a '34 phaeton, that his father helped him build. Two others that stood out were a yellow '40 Tudor sedan and a red deuce Tudor sedan. The deuce ran big-and-little whitewalls and a white vinyl top insert with matching diamond-tufted running boards. A Valley Coachmen club plaque was mounted on the rear bumper. Incidentally, Lon Berger, who originally built my deuce 5-window, was in the Valley Coachmen. My dad

didn't know Lon but remembers seeing my deuce in the early Sixties.

My dad's best friend, Dave "Scotty" Schumway, introduced him to the Violators of Van Nuys. Their red painted and polished aluminum club plaque featured a slingshot dragster with the driver holding the broken-off steering wheel above his head. Even though he didn't join the Violators, my dad still kept tight with his buddy Scotty, who introduced him to his pal Dick McCargue. Dick worked at a used car lot in Van Nuys. Occasionally the lot would have hot rods for sale, and Dick had access to all the car keys. This is how my dad had his first hands-on hot rod experience.

On a Wednesday night, Dick and Scotty "borrowed" a '29 A-V8 roadster pickup from the lot and brought it over to my dad's house. My dad's jaw dropped when he saw the bright red fenderless hot rod. Power was supplied by a 3/4 race '48 Merc motor that was dressed up with Weiand heads and a three-pot manifold topped with Stromberg 97s. Exhaust exited through chrome tubular headers with cutouts. A filled deuce grille shell updated the frontend, while a stock bed was still behind the cab. The Model A frame had the splash aprons intact to hide the frame rails. It rolled on 16-inch steelies wrapped in blackwall motorcycle tires up front and truck tires out back. The interior

I recently found this color transparency in an envelope that was sealed back in '71. It was taken during the *Rod & Custom* photo shoot for the January '71 issue. It was unreal to see it in full color after only seeing it in black and white for the last 30 years! That's me holding the toy T, my mom Myra, and dad Alan. Darryl Norenberg photo.

Top: Another outtake from the *R & C* photo shoot at the Van Nuys airport. Darryl Norenberg photo. **Center**: The T at Dick Ryerson's shop in August, '59. Alan Kahan photo; by '60, dad's hot rod was stored at my mom's parent's house in Los Angeles. Myra Kahan Feely photo. **Bottom**: The T was moved to my dad's parent's garage in North Hollywood, close to Stan Wiesbard, who squirted the coupe's lacquer. Ben Kahan photo; the car after final assembly at Barris, shop in '64. Kahan Archives photo.

featured white vinyl tuck-and-roll with a matching top and tonneau cover. The windshield was chopped to 6 inches high. The capper was the Model A rearend that had a hand painted on the banjo center flipping the bird to all that followed!

The three of them set off on a ride that my dad will never forget. They took off and headed into Tujunga, where they uncorked the headers with borrowed tools at a Tide Water gas station. After exploring the Sunland/Tujunga area they headed into Glendale. The uncorked headers awakened the sleepy streets, and it wasn't long before they noticed a patrol car behind them. The Glendale cop had the light and sirens going, and the chase was on. After making a few quick turns, they pulled into a dark parking lot and hid under the rod. The cops sped by and relief briefly set in until some men in suits approached them. Surprisingly, they just wanted to check out the hot rod. One suit even lent them wrenches to cork the exhaust back up.

They snuck out of Glendale as fast as they could and ended up cruising Hollywood Boulevard and the Sunset Strip, which was just beginning to "happen." They drove into a few underground parking structures to do burnouts for the loud echo effect. Back onto Sunset they tore down the street towards UCLA. When they got close to the college a '55 Cadillac Eldorado pulled up alongside them. The driver had two hot blondes with him. When the light turned green the race was on. Within seconds all they could see were the taillights of the brand new Caddy fading into the distance. Humbled, they headed down Sepulveda Pass and ran out of gas at a tunnel entrance. Luckily they were able to coast all the way down to Ventura Boulevard, where they pulled into an Atlantic-Richfield station, scrounged up 97 cents between the three of them and filled the tank up with three gallons of gas. By the time my dad got dropped

off it was after midnight, way past his curfew. His dad was pissed.

The next morning my dad tried to convince my grandfather to help him buy the hot rod for the asking price of a whopping 500 bucks! Granddad refused, so for the time being Dad occasionally "borrowed" hot rods with his buddies and cruised Van Nuys Boulevard. While hanging out at Bob's Big Boy and the A&W Drive-In, he checked out all kinds of hot rods. Two cars inspired him to build a full-fendered tall T. Both rods were of the '26-'27 variety and sat on heavy "Dagoed" rakes. One was chopped, painted pink, flathead powered, and owned/driven by a chick. The second one was unchopped, gray primered, flathead powered, and ran white steel wheels.

Building a hot rod finally became a reality for my dad in May of '58. One of his buddies told him that their Scout leader was selling an abandoned project. He knew he had to own it when he saw the '24 T coupe body, which had been dragged out of the Mojave Desert a few years earlier. For the grand asking price of $200 he loaded up and took home a completely disassembled '50 Olds motor; side-shifter '39 Cad/LaSalle gearbox that had a Ford tailshaft grafted to it; and some good deuce parts, including a rearend, split front wishbones, the frame and a rare Okie Miller dropped and filled axle. The last thing on the parts list was a set of 16-inch steel wheels.

His first idea was to paint it gold and name it "Goldie the Golden T." But he needed some help putting all the pieces together. At the time my dad didn't have any connections, so he drove to the *Hot Rod* magazine office on Hollywood Boulevard and asked for some advice. They recommended Tom Ikonda's shop, but Tom didn't want anything to do with the project, saying there was no money in building hot rods. He recommended a guy across the street named Dick Ryerson who built Triumph motorcy-

From the top: That's me at age seven and a half standing by dad's T at the Winternationals Rod, Custom, Motorcycle and Race Car show in February '73. Alan Kahan photo; Dick Ryerson rebuilt and hopped up the '50 Olds motor to '54 Olds specs. Photo from the Kahan Archives; participant patch from the '64 Winternationals Custom Auto Fair where Barris debuted the T.

cles and hot rods. Dick owned a '29 Chevy roadster that was powered by a '34 Chev four-banger with an Olds head on it. With some help from my grandpa, my dad negotiated a contract with Dick to build him a running chassis with the body mounted on it for $600. My dad would supply the parts and Dick would get paid when the body and chassis were finished.

Work progressed, but Dad soon realized Dick was a total alcoholic, and the rod ended up being there for two years. Dick built an A frame and stretched it 6 1/2 inches. This allowed the use of the stock firewall and also allowed more leg room. The body was slid back, but the fenders stayed in their stock position. Dick rebuilt and hopped up the '50 Olds 303 motor to 324-inch '54 Olds specs. The motor was bored out and the heads rebuilt with stock valves. My dad took the crank, flywheel, pistons, rods, and bearings to Edelbrock, where everything was balanced. A reground Isky cam was used. Reath automotive sold him in Edelbrock three-two manifold that was fed by 97s. The motor also had a six-volt Mallory Magspark ignition.

Dick built a set of beautiful chrome headers to my dad's specs. They had two outlets on each side because the plan was to run two Model A mufflers and two glasspacks, making it sound like a four banger. By 1960, Dick had completed his part of the build-up, and the T was soon moved to my dad's parent's house in North Hollywood close to painter Stan Wiesbard's house. Five gallons of black Duco lacquer and four gallons of thinner were purchased for $100. The paint job was sprayed in Stan's North Hollywood driveway, and my mom and dad color sanded between coats. Next stop was the Barris shop in North Hollywood where Dick "Korky" Korkies fitted the fenders, and then the final assembly took place. My dad can't remember the name of the guy who did the interior, but he worked out of Barris' shop. Before the T was registered, Barris trailered it to the '64 Winternationals Custom Auto Fair for its debut at the Great Western Exhibit Center in Los Angeles.

In August of '66, Von Dutch striped the T at his Reseda home. Dutch asked my dad what he wanted on it. Knowing about Dutch's erratic temperament he asked Dutch what he thought it needed. Dutch's idea was to stripe it "simple, like an old car." That was exactly what my dad wanted but was a bit scared to ask for. Dutch continually drank wine between pulling lots of straight apple-green lines. I was there, in my mom's tummy, for the six-hour striping session. The cost was $60. Dutch didn't usually sign his striping jobs, but my dad asked him if he would sign this one. Dutch replied, "That will cost you $20." Without hesitation my dad said, "Sign it then." This was probably the best twenty-dollar investment my dad ever made!

After having tons of trouble with the Olds powerplant and LaSalle trans they were

From the top: The California Bear radiator cap was acquired from a "biker type" who said he had the "perfect radiator cap" for my dad's T. Darryl Norenberg photo; dad's "Hard Times" club jacket from the Seventies displayed with the January '71 Rod & Custom feature spread. Photo by Aaron Kahan; Alan Kahan's T at the Throttlers picnic, Burbank, October 2001. Aaron Kahan photo.

Three generations of Kahan hot rodders at the Throttlers picnic in October 2001: dad Alan, grandson Benjamin, and son Aaron, who is a member of Burbank's Choppers. Fred Hildago photo.

yanked out in late '66. A wrecked '65 Ford Mustang with 29,000 original miles donated a 289 motor and C4 trans. They were installed at Blackie's Auto Wrecking on San Fernando Road in Sun Valley. The rod was in its final configuration by '70 when the hood was scratch-built by Morro Bay's Howard Caccia, who eventually sold all his tooling to Rootlieb. When Howard finished the hood, the T was taken back to Dutch, where the hood was striped on saw horses.

My dad's brother-in-law at the time was Robert Williams. Williams and Jim "Jake" Jacobs were totally impressed by my dad's car and teamed up to get it in *Rod & Custom* when they were still working at Roth's. Jake was starting to work for *R&C* and wrote the feature, which appeared in the January 1971 issue.

A lot of my childhood was spent in the T, going to shows and weekend cruising. It was obviously a big influence on my interest in early style hot rods. The T was never completely taken off the road, but had a few hibernation periods after my parents divorced in '72. It was stored over at my grandparents' from '73 to '76. It only saw the

streets for short jaunts to keep it in running order. When I got my hot rod, I bugged my dad for years to get the T out of the garage and enjoy it. It took him a few years to get into the idea that he should have fun and drive his T more often. But with the help of Jerry Lechich of Rod Works Inc., and good friend Jeff Wasserman, it is now fully operational and driven constantly.

I would love to see the car put back to its original configuration. Take off the hood and bumpers. Duplicate the original black and yellow license plate. Add taller tires out back. It would be the ultimate if the Olds motor and Cad/LaSalle box were back in place. The valve covers would be super hard to find because Albertson Oldsmobile of Culver City supposedly made only 10 pairs for their racing cars. Does anyone out there have a set? Of course everything taken off would be kept as part of the car's history. I know it runs and drives great as is, but now that he has a driving '29 roadster, the T could be put back to its first configuration. What do you think dad? Its up to you, but I think it's a bitchin' idea!

VISCERAL AND INSTINCTIVE

By Peter Vincent

TRYING TO PIN DOWN EXACTLY

what defines the visceral, or just plain "gut level" nature of a hot rod and the hot rod culture is not as easy as I thought it would be. Part of the problem is the open nature of hot rodding, with the other part being the viable and very real sensory reaction that comes from the inside of the culture as a participant, as well as from the outside as a spectator. A considerable amount of this definition and reaction comes from the visual part of our senses, but that is definitely not all of it. I am a photographer, and while I relate first to almost everything I see in a visual way, transferring it into two-dimensional photographic images, it is only part of the overall equation.

Hot rods are felt in a way that awakens all of our senses. This can be intellectualized to death by saying that real hot rods have "this part" or "that part," such as Halibrand quick-change rear ends; big and little tire and wheel combinations with, of course, the "right" wheels; or the "correct" engine with the "correct" engine dressing and accessories such as carburetors versus modern injection systems and Roots blowers versus turbos. Everything can be planned and well thought out, with the design being formalized much in the same way that most of the major car companies and high-end car builders rely on. There is intellectual and real value in all of this, with the properties of design, proportioning and advanced design bringing everything together to create a final cohesive unit.

But hot rods come from the gut in an instinctual and visceral way that involves all of our senses. A large amount of our reaction to a hot rod comes from experience and history, and by that I mean our personal experience and history. Many of us grew up with hot rodding as part of our everyday culture. We have developed an aesthetic that comes from the roots of hot rodding, but it also is a culmination of all our physical senses and

Previous page (from the top): Jim Lattin had the McAlister/Walker historic race car at Bonneville during the 50th Anniversary in '98. The car ran at Bonneville in '49; Ron Jolliffe's '49 Olds and Terry Hunt's '53 Studebaker on the salt.

This page (above): Willow Kirk and her '53 Chevy custom at Muroc in 2000; (at right): Tom & Diana Branch at Muroc with their Eddie Dye roadster, which has been since sold to Don Orosco; Steve "Carpy" Carpenter & Drew Pietsch's '28-'29 Dodge roadster, Muroc 2000.

From the top: Eric Perkins' '36 Ford roadster photographed at Bonneville in '92; "Flathead Jack" Schafer's '49 Merc at the Concord Pavillion.

what we have experienced at these levels. It's almost an instinct, the same kind of sense that allows us to separate true fine art from mere decoration.

Everyone has an opinion, including me, as to what turns us on and makes our clock tick. But there does seem to be a universal level that is reached with all the right parts in the right place. You know in your gut that what has been created is a bonified hot rod. When one of these unique cars pulls up next to you, your reaction is visceral, instinctive and emotional. All the senses kick in, and you know at the core of your being that it is a hot rod. The visual nature is sometimes enough, but when you hear the exhaust rumble of an American V-8, especially one with a little compression and a lumpy cam, other senses besides the visual begin to kick in to complete the picture.

The true and ultimate reaction comes from the ride. The view through a chopped windshield, regardless of whether it be a roadster or coupe, is heaven, especially if it

is over a hood punched full of louvers. At this point, all of your senses are aware of what a hot rod is. It is a ride down the black line on the salt of Bonneville, or it is kicking up a dusty rooster tail on the dry lakes of El Mirage or Muroc. But then it could also be a quarter-mile acceleration dash down the local drag strip, or just a late-night cruise on the boulevard listening to the sound of the engine and exhaust reverberating off the surrounding buildings.

One of my all-time favorites is the extended road trip, and I'm not talking "Americruise" or anything organized and part of a group. I'm talking about just you, the car and a lonely desert highway at sunset and after. No distractions. That is when the driver becomes one with the ride; and the freedom of the road accentuates everything that there is to know about the hot rod, and it

From the top: Dennis Kyle and Terry Hegman cruising after the 2000 R.C.R.R. in Kyle's well known (and admired) '32; Keith Tardel and Larry McKenzie's '27 "T" blown flathead Bonneville race car.

comforts, and a straightforward and "to the bones" hot rod is like the difference between night and day. A hot rod offers a visceral avenue into all the senses. There is a connection, and part of it is the knowledge that what you are driving is "cool" and individualistic. It is a statement in itself and it is kinetic. Certain hot rods will do this, and actually it will affect viewers and spectators much in the same way, but driving it is really the best seat in the house.

In the Seventies, it was Chapouris' "California Kid" and Jake's coupe that helped bring back the direction and aesthetic for me. Then Pete Eastwood's "Barakat & Eastwood" red oxide primered '32 drag racing sedan was featured on the cover of *Hot Rod* magazine, and Dick Page's black primered blown and chopped '32 sedan cruising in the Seattle/Tacoma area. I had met Dennis and Debbie Kyle at Bonneville with their orange and much louvered '32 highboy, and from there met Billy Vinther with his straight-on hot rod '34, and Cal Tanaka with his flamed ground-scraping '33, Paul Bos with his '34 McCoy flamed coupe and his '28 roadster

This page (from the top): "Hot Rod Joe" Davis driving home after the 2001 Paso meet; Jake's coupe and Bruce Meyer's Pierson Bros. coupe at the 1996 Muroc Reunion; Terry Hegman and his beatifully proportioned and crafted '51 Merc custom

Opposite page: Cal Tanaka's nasty ground scraping flamed '33 coupe

pickup, and Don Small's right-on-the-money black '32 highboy with the tall "sugar donut" tires.

Ron Jolliffe (who has raced at Bonneville and drives a blown Olds powered '32 highboy) and I were once trying to figure out what it is visually that screams "hot rod," and what pushes the buttons on the nasty and in-your-face feeling that comes from some cars more than others. What we came up with was that it really is hard to put all of this visual dialogue into words. All the cars mentioned above have it, but we both agreed that the nastiest and most in-your-face car was Tanaka's '33 coupe. It wasn't any more of a hot rod than any of the others, but it definitely strikes a presence and it has the lumpy cammed and high compression engine sound to go with it. Of course, all these particular hot rods have that sound. Cal just likes to push the limits in cam and ground-scraping lowness. Each one of these cars strikes a chord, and each is an individual statement and direction, with many of the same parts and ideas used. But most of all, each is different in the way that the finished

form, or hot rod, uses them. Each has its own unique visual direction and makes statements of individuality. Most importantly, they all get driven.

The places that I seem to constantly find cars like these are at the dry lakes and Bonneville, where I also usually run into Vern Tardel and the extended group of hot rodders out of the Santa Rosa and Oakland areas. Then there are the reliability runs, such as the River City Run in December, which gives me a great excuse to bail out of Idaho winter for a few days. Hot rods are part of the environment, and the environment is part of the hot rod, so to speak. The "in-your-face" hot rod attitude doesn't always come off on a fairground venue, especially when you have the car surrounded by lawn chairs. Cruising the boulevard is part of it. Midnight races and desert drives down the lonely two-lane blacktop are ultimately cool and fitting. 🚗

THE PASO PILGRIMAGE

As you could imagine, Anthony Castaneda's (Shifters) bubbletop Model A sure made a stir at Paso. His lime green metalflake "life-size" Hot Wheel could be found at the far end of the park, actually on a perimeter side street where the majority of "real" hot rods migrate.

By Rob Fortier

Even though West Coast Kustom's, annual Cruisin' Nationals in Paso Robles, California, celebrated its twentieth anniversary in 2001, the event simply known as "Paso" didn't really come of age until early in the '90s, when the younger generation of rodders began to really bloom. Paso reached its peak toward the close of the last century, to the point where a cap had to be put on the number of vehicles registered for the show. Simply put, for anyone wanting to see the best of what the West has to offer in the way of nostalgia rods and customs, this was and is the place to be each Memorial Day weekend.

Up until the last few years, the main emphasis of Paso focused on customs, from NorCal's big-name cars to the average little guys' backyard creations. More recently, though, hot rod fever has stirred in the blood of tons of young rodders, even well beyond the California borders. This has resulted in a new "air" to the event, especially on the outskirts or streets surrounding the park where the show is held. A large number of clubs is sprouting up, while the established ones like The Shifters and Choppers keep strengthening their foundations, showing up every year with clever interpretations of the cars from the good old days. For most, there's always a high level of anticipation to see exactly what new cars make Paso each year.

For those who are unfamiliar with the ritual of the Paso weekend, let me put it into perspective. Though some opt to make the trek to the scenic Central California town on Thursday, the action doesn't really kick into gear till Friday. This is where the generations "gap" the activities. While the annual cruise up and down Spring Street (Paso's main drag) sees participants of all ages, the elder rodders tend to gather around the host hotel, the Paso Inn, but the

Rudy Rodriguez's latest, a lower than most '35 Ford pickup, with its heavily hammered top, perfect stance, and tasteful flathead with a high-rise and 94s obscuring occupant's view. The slogan on the side represents the red light district in Tijuana.

local A&W Drive-In is where you'll find the majority of the younger population on hand. In the eyes of the local law enforcement, it's a citation pool, but for anyone wanting to hang out at an actual drive-in burger joint, shoot the breeze with friends from far and wide, and even hear some live rockabilly music, you can't beat it. Back at the Inn, the action is stirring just as well, but maybe at a lower pace.

Sleep deprivation is the key phrase the following morning, as anybody who wants to get a decent spot inside the park has to be up and "in line" way before the crack of dawn. This is one reason why you'll find many of the real hot rods (I'm gonna try and stay away from the "rat rod" term) around the perimeter streets of the park. If you're not in by, say 7 a.m., forget it! The center of the park is where you'll find the high-digit cover customs in all their glory, while many clubs manage to assemble in groups along the fringe. Veteran attendees of Paso know exactly where to go to find the different types of rods and customs, as it's sort of a "healthy segregated" show. But for newcomers, the

From the top: Some of the hot rods that make Paso are literal barn hibernation revivals, with speed equipment and hard-to-find goodies that most endlessly scour the swaps for. Nevertheless, it's great to see old-time iron, regardless of where it originated; Paso Friday night means the A&W Drive-In at the end of town for most, even while the cruise down Spring Street is going on. No bobby socks or carhop service here...just plenty of cool hot rods, customs, and b.s.'n till the joint shuts down.

Von Franco's '27 T, a very close copy of Ray Andereg's coupe-turned-roadster from the late '50s, made Paso with not a moment to spare. Franco literally burned the midnight oil on this project, but made the show just in time to display his latest, candy gold creation.

entire show is probably the greatest potpourri of what this hobby has to offer that you'll ever encounter. Off one of the side streets is what you might call vendor row, where you can find hard parts and accessories (and probably everything in between) from folks like Mooneyes and Gene Winfield, art and collectibles from Dennis McPhail and the Roth Brothers, or clothing from a host of outfits.

Saturday night is again, for the most part, a separation of the ages. In the city park, West Coast Kustoms stages a free concert with great live bands, and that's where you'll find those looking for more of a family fun type evening. On the other end of the spectrum, literally, is the annual Shifters Show. Held at different locations over the years (for various reasons, use your imagination), this past year saw the gig staged at the bowling alley on the far end of town. Live music over the years has ranged from original doo-wop acts to rockabilly bands like Big Sandy and even The Paladins. Like the A&W scene, this is an event where cops keep a close eye on

things, but everybody has an amazing time, and the fun doesn't usually stop till the wee hours of the morning.

Unlike Saturday's show in the park, Sunday is more relaxed—no dawn-patrol racing to get a good spot in line. Some choose to forgo the park altogether and get an early jump on their trips back home, while others enjoy a less crowded atmosphere under the trees, most sticking around for the awards ceremony later in the afternoon. Nonetheless, it's a night-and-day difference from the crazy scene of the previous day.

So there you have Paso in a nutshell. For me, it's a yearly experience I greatly look forward to, especially the adventure of the drive up the coast. It's the only place where I may see certain friends each year, but more importantly, a place where I get to see all the different cliques of the hobby unite for a weekend. Some may be there for the "scene," while others make the Paso Pilgrimage for one thing: the cars.

HOP UP
Magazine
5-WINDOW
BUILD UP

C·CRUZ ©/999

FINAL REPORT: IT LIVES!!!

Top: Jay starts all the slicin' and dicin' after careful layout and consideration of the extra half-inch cut. **Bottom**: Top is dropped back on for the "50-foot" test.

Down to the short strokes. We got the thing plumbed and the running gear all in it; the brakes are made up, radiator, starter and generator (yeah), and the body is on the frame.

And now the big one. We drug the wreck over to the Kennedy Bros. for the ax. It is done without shame. Without remorse. Without looking back or even considering for one flat second whether or not we are ruining a good uncut Fiver. It's done with a single mindedness and satisfaction that, well, it needed doing, Boys.

It was decided to go a little lower than the 2 1/2 to 3 inch norm. We had as a model a full fendered car that had been cut 4 inches. Looked pretty extreme. Real low, it ought to do fine. We went back to three and a half and are totally pleased. The extra half inch causes geometric and mechanical challenges that Jason Kennedy found labor intensive but easy, intellectually.

We brought the heap back and every other part you can think of is in the barn and all you gotta do is assemble. Day and frickin' night. And then some.

We took all those gauges that Carburetor Joe donated, hogged out holes in the dash, and added some nice switches. We mounted the new (old) Bell wheel, and then—get this —we called in Swell Tom (trim guy from Canoga) and said we wanted to "save that blown-out t 'n' r" that had been in the hulk when we found it. He could do it with patches, repairs, tape, stitching, gluing, stretching and all, but he said it "wouldn't stay together." "How 'bout those clear plastic covers?" He laughed and, Whoa Daddy! You can see in the photos that the interior is the same one that was in it in the late Fifties.

Top to bottom: Final rear lowering, reinstallation of 50's nerf bars and a hundred other steps remain even after it starts to look like a car again; Century auto glass made a house call. There had been a blue plexiglass windshield in the frame—a vestigal element of the coupe's drag racing life; Swell Tom went out of his way to save an interior that was thought to be good only for the patterns. You gotta see it!

L.A. Ray punched the rear lid full of louvers (his die matches that of E. Rick Vaughn who had punched the four-piece hood for another project years before) and we were properly ventilated. The Kennedys bobbed the rear fenders and the sheetmetal was done in mostly original prime, which still has traces of the "Surgers Racing Team-Glendale" signage on the doors and "Crower Roller Cams" on the cowling. A little Fifties orange paint radiates through here and there in the haze. That will be the paint color if/when the car gets to that.

The final steps are: wiring, throttle linkage, speedo cable and all that rot that seems to take longer than it oughta. The coupe did not get done in time for Bonneville as planned, but as of this writing is a runner...

And all without shameless plugs for advertisers' products (some of which found their way on to the car anyway, but we can't brag about them or you might think we got them free). Trust us, Daddy-Os. No free parts. Just a hell of a lot of fun, which is only outdone by—the run.

This is truly a great land.

Top: The original Eddie Dye Custom Roadster; **Right**: New nose was made with original nose present for pattern-making.

t's happenin,' Boys. DBO is pressing on the Eddie Dye roadster.

The car was missing from our awareness for many years, and it's identification by Hop Up Guys as a rolling and running remain was cited in the first two *Hop Up* Annuals. It's arguably the best example of a 1950's custom roadster and, if not, it absolutely keeps company with only one or two ahead of it, namely Neicamp and Flint in one order or another. Y'all can probably add others in your own order of preference and meaningfulness.

Since Stryker has made floors, pans and the nose, the DBO craftsmen have something to work around and attach to the rest of the car, which was recently acquired from another Hop Up Guy, Tom Branch. It was Branch and Kevin Preciado (Cyclone) who ID'd the car as the Dye roadster. Leave it to our kin, Boys.

First daylight for the car will most likely be at Pebble Beach in '03—where customs will be featured in the alternating-year program that allows our kind of scrappers to compete with one another among the blue-bloods—and we're pretty sure that *Hop Up* 2004 (Volume V) will have a color feature on it (again scooping the Big Boys) or at least the freshest build-up notes available.

We get the nod because, well...we're *Hop Up*, Man.

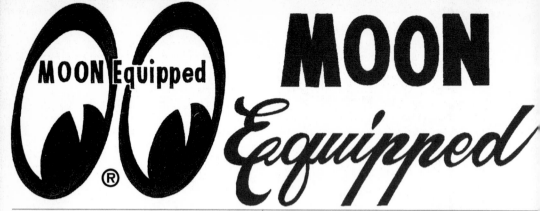

MALTESE CROSS ACCESSORIES

Motorcycle
Mirror
#GT003IC
$39.95 Ea

Inner Rear View Mirror
#GT002IC $39.95 Ea

Side View
Peep Mirror
#GT001IC..$39.95 Ea

#AA111IC..Air valve caps..$8.50 Set of 4
#AA112IC..Door Locks......$6.50 Pr
#AA113IC..License Bolts...$4.50 Pr

Iron Cross
Hat#CM037 $15

*REMEMBER KIDS.
IT'S NOT WHO YOU ARE,
IT'S WHAT YOU WEAR!*
- RYAN

ICE COOLER

Solid metal construction
with movable locking
handles.#MQG16
$ 139.00

BARSTOOL

Black vinyl seat with
white imprint.#MQMG292

$84.95 Ea

LONG SLEEVE SHIRTS

Front

M, L, XL, XXL $25.00 Ea
Choose from 2 styles   Back →

#MQTL018   #MQTL012

MECHANICS JACKET

Can Cooler
#MG091BKIC $3.00

Cotton. Black M,L,XL,XXL
#MQW001 $125.00 Ea

MOON EQUIPPED WOOL JACKET

Embroidered rear logo. Black #MQW002 $298.00

Catalog
$3

ZIPPO

#MQG019
$25.00 Ea

ANTENNA BALL

#MG015IC
$2.00 Ea

IRON CROSS STICKER
#DM082S 3" $3
#DM082L 5" $5

ROADSTER
STICKER
#MQD006BK $3

White Wall
Slicks available
Call

Call 800-547-5422 562-944-6311
Fax 562-946-2961 www.moonequipment.com
10820 S. Norwalk Blvd Santa Fe Springs, CA 90670

Archives

Wonder if someday they'll dry up. There weren't all that many guys doing this stuff over the ages, and all of their scrapbooks and shoeboxes full of pictures are being mined for gems by all the real magazine guys...and this ragged-ass little excuse for a publishing company still seems to get its share. How's that?

Maybe we just have good Pals.

This chapter includes warm looks at outdoor hot rod shops in farmland, photos of notorious people and cars taken by not-notorious people (Hop Up Guys), and as is the case these days, some of the included pieces are photos of photos and whatever else it takes to share the anthropology of our community of hairy-legged hot rodders.

Stolen By
STROUPE!

"Commander" Stroupe of the Northern Front seems to sniff out rare photos that even the keenest snoops have not snooped. Maybe it's his definitive moto-detective skills or simply that he has a *way* with widows. Consider that when you are leaving your instructions.

Notable on the opposite page is the slender feller to our left: a young Dean Moon posing next to his roadster with—probably—no inkling of the impact he'd make in his chosen fields of endeavor and play. Or was it vice-versa?

Opposite page (from the top): Bonneville signage from the Forties; Dean Moon with his unstroked Mercury—is this a preview of the Moon fuel block?
This page (from the top): Isky's car with its trademark V-8 engine with maxi overdrive and homemade valve covers—he still owns it!; Tony Grippo's '29 pickup on Deuce rails—note the Tattersfield heads and the bedrail exhaust.

This page (from the top): At the dry lakes—a heavily louvered car with Bonneville Tires, quick change and eight pipes; the modified on the left is still our favorite modified of all time—(next to the two in this issue!). This is what it looked like when Doug Caruthers owned it. Chrisman stretched it, and it became the first digger to go 140, then all hell broke loose with it. It ran both T and B motors in its earlier lives.

Opposite page (from the top): Two shots from the backstage of Oakland Speedway. We like the '36 tow car (taildragger) and the T roadster roundy car with high-tech knock-off wheels. This outfit probably equates to a full Kodiac-equipped race effort of today; a '26-'27 Chevy roadster.

W̲e at Hop Up have always been lucky to have friends. Cause it's been from pals, like Aussie Steve, where we seem to get the best stuff to share with you.

The photos you see here are just a portion of Aussie Steve's vast archives. You see, Steve is one of those guys who's always the first at a swap meet, always early for the lit shows, and he comes away with the choicest material. Plus, Steve's collection benefits from a deep knowledge of not only the cars, but also the people who drove them.

Consider this a taste, of what Steve has in his collection. We'll bring you more in future annuals.

Opposite page: Bonneville 1952, Eddie Millersix-cylander powered lakester gets a push through the pits.

This page (from the top): A man and his machine at the dry lakes. Ralph Schenk and his lakester. Loosely based on Barney Oldfield's Golden Submarine; Charles "Scotty" Scotts '29 highboy at the dry lakes in 1948. Scotty built the well known Ardun T roadster and Scotty's Muffler Shop belly tank.

Opposite page (from the top): Blackie Gold and his buddy in his '32 roadster; Fred Carillo's rear engine T modified. Running an Evans equipped modified. Car is now in Maryland under restoration.

This page (from the top): Trophy presentation at Bonneville in 1952 for the Class B Streamliner record at 230.16 mph. Won by the City of Burbank Streamliner; The Hilborn Lakester when it was owned by T.E. Warth; 1952 trailer and tow car technology at Bonneville.

From the top: The Lee Chapel Streamliner. It set the class C record at Bonneville in 1952, at 224.114 mph. Car ran an overhead valve conversion of Lee's own design; one of the many belly tanks that ran at Bonneville in the 1950's; Frank Kurtis' "Kurtis Kraft" prototype at Bonneville in 1949. Car ran 142.5 MPH.

T'N'A

It all started here, didn't it now?

Po' boys first had Ts to hop up, then their heirs-apparent did it to As and...like that. What they did was creative, and although progress caused what they did to become obscure for a while, Hop Up Guys are re-enacting the pleasure. The vibration. And, Gawd! Can they vibrate!

We count among our Pals some of the foremost experts in both T and A enjoyment, and in this chapter we get a look at some of their foolishness.

America is truly a wonderful place.

Photo: Darryl Spurlock

MILD MOD
Of
MARIN

MITCH ALLEN RAISES THE BAR FOR MODIFIED MACHINATION

E lsewhere in *Hop Up* 2002 we have seen the nicely turned-out modified T roadster of Jeff Chiodo. We appreciated the aesthetic touches and the spirit behind the quintessential banger-powered modified— all painted up in the final incarnation of the design processes of the builder. Not too many in the old days got to the final version.

Now, enter Mild Mitch Allen, and the ebony/ivory, yin/yang, ee-ther/eye-ther, to-may-to/to-mah-to, polar opposite of the same dang thing. It is NOT unfinished. Although it could get paint, plate and trim in another life, this life is fulfilled. Done. Evolved to the last molted, skin-shedding version.

A long-time hot rod cat and Hop Up Guy, The Mild One was ready to take on another build project, and it was certain that it had to be a banger-modified. The experience, though, had to be as much a part of it as the use of the finished car. He decided that the car had to be built entirely at home, employing all the skills he had accumulated to date...and some he had yet to acquire. Mitch thought that the barnyard engineering done in the day, and so rare today because modern

communications have us so proximate to problem solvers and parts, would have to be a great experience.

He done good.

Starting with a '32 Ford truck cab of questionable lineage, and an A frame, The Mild One began to lay the gow out, and lay it out, and lay it out. Some things are just hard to get laid out concisely. But he persevered, and the rod took on a unique character based on Mitch's hot rod intellect, good eye and, well, months of fitting, grinding, welding and filing...and further laying out!!!

The top of the cab became the belly pan. Of course! The outside tops of the window openings became the patch panels for the cowling and cockpit tops. Of course. An old Cornbinder Travelall project donated the swing pedals—conventional Ford pedals were not going to fit, and "Hey! Look at them thangs!!!"

A Franklin steering gear from an old midget racer, complete with perfect-sized three-spoke Bell wheel, covered the aiming

chores, coupled with a stock '34 axle and spring in front, the '32 truck 'bones, '46 rearend (stock width) with both front and back axles hung on Bulldog Perches. Rollers are 16x4-inch steelies in front ('40 brakes) and 16-inch Ford wires on the rear, slowed down with the '46 brakes. B engine, '39 box, and a severely shortened torque tube and drive shaft complete the drivetrain.

You hafta agree that this unit has all the stance, attitude and charisma of the best of them. And a patinaed charm that you cannot build in to a new one. But it does. It does.

Then the big debut day arrived: the 2001 Auburn, California, Model A (B and T) Hillclimb. They flat-tow the cool mod with the Garlits-like '69 Chrysler wagon tow rig, proceed to shake everybody to the ground with the cool look and...*Madre de Dios!* He jumps up and wins his class at the races. Then at the Antique Nationals he ran hard and broke out of his bracket in the third round and Lordy knows what's next?

Not paint we'll bet.

Opposite page (from the top): Mitch pulls out for his first run at Auburn, California Hillclimb; nose is positioned to accommodate a hood in some future incarnation; perch, friction shocks, 'bones, King Bees are de rigueur for any period modified roadster.

This page (from the top): Hand fuel pressure pump is aesthetic—everything else is purely purposeful; the Mild Mod at a rare moment of rest between Hillclimb runs.

Text & Photos by Drew Hardin

Every once in a while, even in a hustle-bustle city like Los Angeles, you sometimes turn a corner and step back in time. For instance, when you stand in Jeff Chiodo's driveway and look past his bungalow into the barely two-car garage that sits behind it, you have to remind yourself that you're still in the 21st century. For sharing that small space is a tidy 5-window Model A and a bright yellow T modified. SCTA timing tags hang on the garage wall, as do an assortment of racing posters. A World War II-era tool chest, hand-lettered with bomber-nose art, sits on the well-used work bench. You could swear you were back in post-war America, visiting a buddy who was getting ready for a lakes meet.

But what you're looking at is a modern-day mix of the authentic past and the revisited past. The authentic Forties gear — the timing tags and tool chest — belonged to Jeff's grandfather, Elmer. Elmer was an aviation engineer who worked on Jack Northrop's Flying Wing during the war years. He also tinkered with hot rods. Elmer was around when the SCTA was forming, and he earned those tags piloting a number of '32s on the dry lakes.

Spanning the past and present is the A, a car Jeff has owned since he was a teenager. Back then he drove it to high school. It has since been restored and sits, under cover, waiting for its next Sunday drive.

The T modified is the past revisited. It's a mix of repop and good old stuff, and its overall design was modeled after those pre-war rods that set the stage for the hop up boom to come. "This was a difficult project because I wanted everything to look like the

Above: Gilmore red and yellow are an homage to Jeff's grandfather Elmer and his board-track racing days. **Lower left**: Strand components supplied the hairpins and dropped axle, while Jeff mounted the quarter-elliptic springs on the top side of the frame to give the little T a bit of a rake. **Lower right**: Model A lights are hooked up to turn with the front tires.

From the top: The T modified shares space with Jeff's resto Model A in a time-warp garage; it's a snug fit, huh Jeff?; Willy's Upholstery stretched leather over 3/8-inch steel rod to form the seats.

period," Jeff said. "It would have been a lot easier to take some short cuts, but things just wouldn't have looked right in the end."

So Jeff spent over three years collecting the right parts to add to his reproduction '27 T body and frame. What he couldn't find he made himself, just as his granddad did back in the day. And to honor Elmer's spirit—as well as the laps Elmer took on southern California's board tracks—he painted the T in bright "Roar with Gilmore" colors. Painted it right in that cramped little garage, where he did all the other work on the T.

Lift the modified's aluminum hood and you'll find classic 'banger tech: a '28 Model A block with a counter-weighted B crank and a B grind on the cam. Those are Stromberg 94s on the down-draft intake manifold, as they "were easier to get the car running than 97s," Jeff told us. The exhaust system was custom made and gives the 'banger a nice, throaty sound.

Behind the motor is a lightened flywheel, a clutch out of a Mustang and a '39 Ford trans. The shortened torque tube runs to a

Model A rearend filled with 3.78 gears. Linking the axle to the T bucket is a Model A transverse spring pack without the top three springs, courtesy of Posies. The juice brakes are '40-'41 vintage, and the wheels are Kelsey Hayes wires. Up front, Jeff mounted the repop axle on quarter-elliptic springs that were attached to the top side of the frame to give the T a bit of a rake.

Jeff likes to call his T a "zip-code car," meaning "ya don't go far out of your zip code in it." We wondered why, until we took a look in the cockpit. The '32 dash is cool, as is the three-spoke Bell wheel. But that leather-over-steel-rod seat can't be comfortable over the long haul.

Then again, it can't be that bad. Jeff does drive the car, within and outside of his zip code. He took it to the Throttler's Picnic and the Antique Nats last year, and he likes to tool around town with his young daughter, Ana, at his side. Ana loves the T and helped Jeff with the build, even at the tender age of 3. It looks like Elmer's spirit has taken root in yet another generation.

From the top: Custom exhaust gives the T a nice snarl; 'banger is out of a '28 A and runs a B crank and a B-grind cam, a re-pop Winfield head and Stromberg 94s on the down-draft intake; Jeff made his own "gauge" for the '19 T gas tank. The stop light is from, of all things, a Hupmobile.

Top: Straw's T Touring body was among a car load of T parts being sold in a pal's driveway sale. (One guy came a day late, Ed.) **Left to right**: The rest of the car—from rad shell to diff—is a "probably runs OK" A-Bone. Turned out just fine; Hop Up sticker is focal point of the windshield art; that's wet salt sliming the cowling and 'shield.

CAR
asis On Stupid!)

As we have seen, gow is accomplished in a lot of ways. Early on, one combo was the literal T 'n' A: T body on later A chassis. This one is dear to us because we wanted the body shown here when it came up for sale, but got there a day late (you know the rest) and it had been pledged to someone higher up the rust food chain.

Steve Straw was the cat what got our "favorite car in the whole world," and, if we do say so ourselves, it could not have met a better fate. At Bonneville last year, Straw and another Hop Up Guy, Duane Kofoed, ran the Bejesus outa that car, doing SCTA projects as mundane as clearing debris from the long course to transporting Straw to his job as Impound (Record) Tech Inspector. At Speedweek people expose lots of film on street iron, and this scrapper was the darlin' of the annual revival.

Steve got the body, complete with a nice tufted interior, from P. Wood (See California Bobber elsewhere here in *Hop Up* 2002), and was bent on a low-buck, early gow experience. See, Straw has done it "all" over the years, but Ts figure to him way toward the top of his mechano-fancy. A nice, clean A chassis was used with a stock "probably runs good" motor; some rattle can color, new top (practical choice since the car was intended for his real employment in the B-ville sun), and a tasteful load of stickers and doo-dads. Ya gotta accessorize.

What was wrought here was a true bargain basement, sweat-equity bundle of laughs: practical in a typically perverse Hop Up kinda way. A crowd pleaser. Inspired foolishness, so much so that Mrs. Straw calls it the "Stupid Car." Emphasis on Stupid.

Don't ya love it?!

Joe's T, then and now. That's Joe's cousin, stylin' in the straw hat back in 1950, looking for all the world like he just quaffed that row of brewskis sitting on the Rajo head. Joe's in the lower photo, 81 years young, and enjoying the T now as much as Cuz did back then.

JOE ARRIETA'S

'26 TOURING

T he old photo here depicts Joe Arrieta's older cousin—in 1950—in his defunct T touring car. It had been his gow in the late Twenties, a car that Joe, who was 10 years younger, had coveted along with the roaring lifestyle that the owner had. It had raced at "Jeffries Barn" where semi-organized roundies took place on weekends. They had even beat Floyd Roberts there, who was later an AAA standout. Braggin' rights. Yeah, buddy.

Even in '50, Cuz looks like a Happening Dude, what with his Moon Doggie hat, the empty Miller bottles lined up on the Rajo head and an air of abandon we seem to detect in the earliest hot rodders. By now Joe had grown to "beer-peer" status; and he'd become a nag, too. "When you gonna give me the Ford?" he continually asked his Tin-Kin.

In 1953.

Joe got around to the restoration in the early Seventies (ya hafta be dedicated to store something that long), and the quality of the car's finish reflects the era. The engine was rebuilt, got a C Crank, balanced C Rods, aluminum pistons, VW oil pump, and the same cross-flow Rajo head that supported the beer jugs in the picture. There's a downdraft Winfield "S" carburetor and manifold on the induction side, while custom

headers lead to a 4-inch Blooey Pipe and cut-out at the end. The cut-out is really a cut-in, since Joe always runs the thing wide open and cuts it in when "the cops are around." (The gurgling sound will make a believer out of the most cynical 350-350-9 guy.) The Ruxstell two-speed rear axle was obligatory in a full gow job. Honda front disc brakes and modified '57 Chev drums on the rear coupled to homemade backing plates make the thing "Whoa" as good as it'll "Go," and these items make the car a freeway worthy cruiser. The finish quality is exceptional, and the T has clearly been maintained with patient, loving care.

This is iron. It's hot iron and has been such almost since it was new, and it's owner-restorer-caretaker has been with it all the way, spanning virtually the entire life of our hot rod history. And he enjoys the dickens out of it on a daily basis. At 81.

This swindle keeps folk young, ya know?

From the top: Freeway-worthy Flivver has been maintained with lots of loving care; engine sports the same Rajo head that held up the Miller bottles years ago; Joe moved the T's throttle off the column to a spoon-shaped pedal next to the T's other three.

STEERING COLUMNS FOR REAL HOT RODS!

Finally, a rugged steering column without tilts or billet gadgets! Heavy-duty bearings at each end (no plastic bushings), 1 3/4-inch fits popular column drops, 3-bolt wheels fit with no adaptor, standard 3/4-inch - 36-spline end. Clean and simple, like hot rods used to be!

Steel Column $145.

Our NEW Forty-style column $229.95
Beautiful metal-spun cone, shaft has correct key and taper for '40 Ford wheel. Its time has come!

Stainless steel column $175.

Acknowledgments

The cliché "labor of love" applies here. Coco Shinomiya and Drew Hardin have to be part of it or it wouldn't be it.

Preferential treatment by readers, contributors, advertisers and professional colleagues give Hop Up its extra pound of requisite boost. Those visceral gifts make Hop Up what you see in this and the previous two Annuals, and they are the elixir that makes something of nascent dreams of nostalgia and need.

See ya next year. We'll be the ones in the cheap sunglasses.

Read Hop Up Every Month at: www.hopupmag.com!

COMING IN VOLUME FOUR

Here's a preview of a few of the things we're working on for HOP UP IV:

Top (right to left): Snapshots from Aussie Steve's Archives.

Left: Ed Donato's 1930 Model A roadster. Donato was a member of the Slow Freights of Watts in the early Fifties.